TOTAL STRATEGY

—•—

RAKESH SONDHI

TOTAL STRATEGY

RAKESH SONDHI

Airworthy Publications
International Limited

First published in 1999 in Great Britain by
Airworthy Publications International Limited,
Bassfield South, Manchester Road,
Walmersley, Bury, Lancashire BL9 5LY.

Copyright © Rakesh K. Sondhi

ISBN 0 952 8845-1-8

To my family, my life

Rakesh K. Sondhi, BSc (Hons), MSc, MBA, MInstMgt

Rakesh Sondhi is a practising strategist with 17 years' experience in many industry sectors including aviation, financial services, agricultural machinery and food. His engineering background developed an analytical and questioning mind which he has successfully utilised for solving strategic level problems.

He is part of the the Associate Faculty at Henley Management College, running strategy sessions for MBA and senior management programmes.

As Managing Director of BMC Associates, Rakesh has advised companies of all sizes worldwide in many different industry sectors. His approach is based on being pragmatic in analysis and creative in identifying solutions.

Rakesh's experience includes the editorship of *ConCISe*, a specialist newsletter about aerospace in the CIS. Other publications include numerous case studies and *Business Improvement through Learning and Transformation* and *Customer Care and Globalisation*.

ACKNOWLEDGEMENTS

I would like thank everyone who has supported my efforts, in particular to Viv and Steve for ensuring my inputs were presentable. I would also like to thank Chris Parker for his contribution to chapter 8 and proof reading the final draft of the book. A special thank you to everyone at Henley Management College for providing the motivation to learn and develop.

Finally, I would like to dedicate the book to my motivation for living – my family – my wife Suman, my children Arjun and Nikisha, my mum and dad, and my sisters and their families, and to my team.

I hope all readers find this work useful and enjoyable.

Contents

List of Figures

Section A

INTRODUCTION

1

DEFINING THE STRATEGIC PROCESS AND A CORPORATE STATE

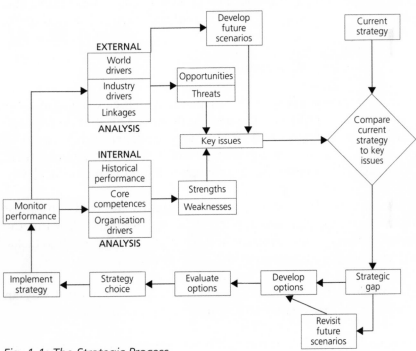

Fig. 1.1: The Strategic Process

"Strategy is when you are out of ammunition, but keep on firing so that the enemy won't know."
Unknown

INTRODUCTION

Aim of the book

The aim of this book is to:
1   provide a basis for holistic strategic thinking
2   encourage creativity in the strategic process
3   create understanding and learning within an organisation.

Strategy is a way of thinking. The process needs to be creative and practical. In addition, a holistic or total approach is required to:

1   identify sources of leverage
2   create long-term advantage.

The development of a strategy is dependent on the quality of analysis and the rigour applied to the strategic process. This process needs to ensure that all angles and perspectives are taken into account to develop a creative strategy that provides sustainable competitive advantage. The analysis needs to be carried out in a methodical way.

The suggested process *(Fig 1.1)* is designed to ensure the most rigorous techniques are applied in a creative way, allowing the development of a more unique and advantageous approach to tackle the challenges of the competitive environment.

By taking each perspective into account in a methodical way an organisation can identify all key assumptions of its business.

This book will take you through the strategic process step-by-step. Each chapter reflects a key stage of the process, which will be highlighted on the process map at the beginning of the chapter. Each chapter is divided into a section on Concepts, Analytical Steps and a Summary mind map. A range of activities are also provided to practise some of the techniques.

The Concepts gives an overview of the theoretical background to the issue under review. A step-by-step guide to carrying out the analysis ensures a rigorous process, with a summary mind map providing a resumé of the chapter.

A simple input-output diagram at the beginning of each chapter defines the purpose of the chapter. Plus there will be a copy of the process map, with the relevant box for the current chapter blackened. All sections of the process that have been completed will be shaded, thus providing an ongoing status of the strategy process.

Philosophy

Today's environment is dynamic and changing rapidly, therefore a company needs to understand this to progress forward. The organisation should be comparable to the free flowing movement of water. As water is able to flow into gaps and cracks, organisations should be able to take advantage of gaps in their markets, i.e. opportunities. Water does not make the decision to flow into the gap: it is in fact "forced" to, due to its composition and make up. Similarly, there is no reason why an organisation's structure cannot "force" itself to take advantage of opportunities.

In addition, the composition of water also "forces" it to divert itself away from obstacles or threats, never needing to face them head on.

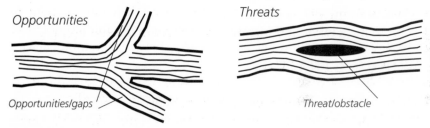

The way water does this is to alter its speed of motion to move around the obstacle.

Thus, it is imperative that successfully structured organisations will never face threats, competition, etc., head on, but will manoeuvre around the threat by altering a variable that represents a strength. This requires excellent intelligence gathering to predict movement.

A criticism of this model may be that water may flow into many gaps, which it may not be able to fill, i.e. spreading its available resources too thinly. This is overcome by the organisation through its strategy-making process. The organisation needs to ensure that its vision and mission are broad enough to take advantage of optimal market size, and its objectives are focused enough to ensure that the organisation is equipped to achieve an optimum market share.

Based on the supposition that an optimum market share is achievable, the organisation will ensure its resources are sufficient to flow into the opportunities. If, however, this is not feasible, then the organisation has two options:

1 Control the entry into the opportunity. The consequence is that people lose their creativity and ability to deliver empowered decisions.
2 Revisit the mission and objectives. This involves, perhaps, focusing on a smaller market niche. This will ensure the people within the organisation are empowered to take advantage of opportunities.

To take the water analogy further, it becomes clear that the source of water to fill the gaps can come from anywhere, but is perhaps driven by a sense of purpose. This means that the organisation needs to have people empowered to make decisions.

Some critical implications of this are:

- training and development
- recruitment
- management and hierarchies of individuals and groups.

WHAT IS STRATEGY?

There are many definitions of strategy. This is one of those terms that people use in many different contexts. Sun Tzu, the Chinese military general, from 3000BC, defined strategy in terms of five key elements. These were:

1. Tao or doctrine of the organisation
The tao is the way of the organisation. This word loses much in translation from its Chinese origins, but essentially means the culture or values and beliefs of an organisation. The tao represents the internal workings of the organisation, and the glue that gels the group of people together into an effective team.

2. Nature
Nature refers to the environment of the organisation. This includes the elements of the world and industry that relate to the business concerned. The environment or nature represents the boundaries of the organisation, including its competitors.

3. Situation
This is the current position of the organisation or its current strengths and weaknesses, particularly in relation to the environment. In order to progress forward, in strategic terms, the organisation needs to establish its current position. This is a snapshot and will be changing continuously.

4. Leadership
The role of leadership is vital in ensuring progress against objectives is met, through the motivation of individuals and communication within the team.

5. Art
One of the key attributes of the leadership is having the ability to change the strategy as the environment dictates. This means that there should be little emotional attachment to the goals or outcomes of a strategy. Decision making needs to be based on complete evaluation of the current situation.

In its simplest terms, strategy can be depicted by *Fig. 1.2*. Strategy is about an organisation's ability to utilise its strengths and weaknesses to take advantage of the opportunities and overcome the threats facing the business. Strategy is about balancing the internal factors with the external drivers of the business.

The art of strategy is therefore about managing conflict
- within the organisation
- within the external environment
- with the competition, and
- among the leaders.

Strategy is a broad and general plan developed to reach long term objectives, focusing on actions for each of the functional areas.

The imperatives of the strategy are shown in *Fig. 1.3*.

DEFINING STRATEGY AS VISIONS AND MISSIONS

Strategy can be expressed in terms of the visions, missions, objectives and tactics. This is the translation of the strategy into meaningful terms for the benefit of employees, customers and all other stakeholders.

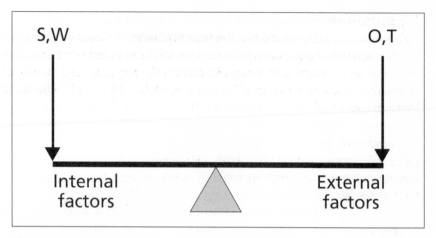

Fig. 1.2: What is strategy?

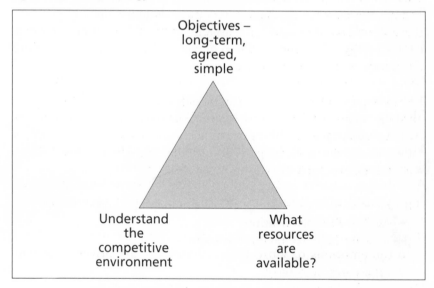

Fig, 1.3: Imperatives of strategy

Visions

Vision means "to see". A vision empowers individuals through the provision of knowledge or expectations of the future, by focusing on a goal.

A vision is an expression of a common set of values in a way that is likely to inspire its people. Sir John Harvey Jones, television's Trouble-shooter and former Chief Executive of ICI, defines vision as follows:

*"An **attractive** and **clear** view of the **future**
which can be **shared**. It must **motivate**, be
ambitious, and should **stretch** people to **achieve**
more than they thought possible."*

David Kirk, the former captain of the New Zealand All Blacks, provides the following explanation of visions:

*"Visions must be **rational**, but they must be
emotional. They are often **distant**. They must
engage and **frighten**. They must be **big**. Leaders
of potential world class teams ask for **sacrifices** that
are immense. There has to be a reason for asking.
Only a vision can **unite** and **invoke** at the highest
level."*

The key words from above are:

Clear view of the future – the vision needs to be easy to understand and easy for its recipients to see the future being aimed for.
Shared – the vision needs to be shared and believed by all of the people in the organisation.
Motivate – visions are the vehicle to motivate and inspire individuals to achieve more than otherwise would be possible.
Ambitious and stretch – visions should be something that force you to push yourself that little bit further, without necessarily ever reaching the ultimate goal.
Rational and emotional – commitment is gained through latching onto the emotions of individuals. Identifying the drivers that will switch the commitment on.
Engage and frighten – fear ensures maximal performance. There is a boundary where fear can have a negative impact on performance. However, fear is also a prerequisite for gaining a competitive edge.

Mission statements

Mission means "to send". Mission statements empower individuals by providing a force which directs individuals in a particular direction, by focusing on a behaviour.

Mission statements can have two purposes:

1   External Public Relations, and
2   Staff motivation

Mission statements can say a variety of things, including:

- broad statements of business activity
- specific outline of the quality, attributes, products or market that the business is involved in
- management's view of the company's capability
- systems or styles of carrying out the business activity

The origins of the mission statement go back to the 1960s, when Levitt introduced the notion of marketing myopia, referring to businesses having very narrow business definitions. For example, Levitt mentioned the railroad company which saw its business as moving people rather than railroading. He suggested that companies should focus the mission on customer needs, or benefits sought, rather than production or technology processes.

In the 1970s, Drucker also stated that businesses need a clear definition of what business the company was in, backed up with specific objectives and strategies.

The components of a mission statement are:

Purpose – this is the primary justification for the existence of the company. Focus is on customers, suppliers, products, services and location.
Principle business aims – these aims may be stated in terms of market share, profitability etc.
Corporate identity – the statement may have an identity it wants to be related to.
Company policies – based on the philosophy, and style of leadership.
Values – the values of the stakeholders related to the business.

The mission statement should be developed when a company is successful. Drucker states that "success always obsoletes the very behaviour that achieved it". As a company tries to maintain its successful position, there is a tendency to forget the values and practices that were largely responsible for the success in the first place.

Fig. 1.4 shows the different types of mission statement.

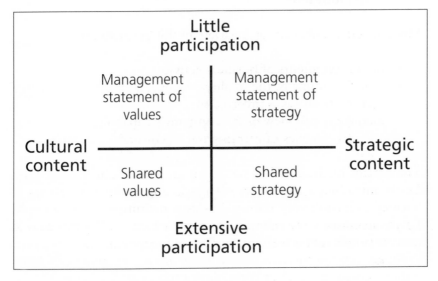

Fig. 1.4: Mission types

The two variables that determine the type of strategy reflected in the mission are:

1   participation, and
2   content.

Participation is the degree of involvement of the people within the organisation. To what extent is there involvement at the lower levels of management?

Content is dependent on the emphasis of the strategy, whether it be focused on the harder elements of strategy or the softer elements of culture.

These different types of mission allow the organisation to develop statements that are meaningful and fulfil the objectives of the exercise. Organisations have to seriously question the value of articulating mission statements that employees have to remember through the use of cards and other visual means, rather than fully committing to a set of values that they believe in.

Corporate and subsidiary missions can have quite different purposes. *See Fig. 1.5.*

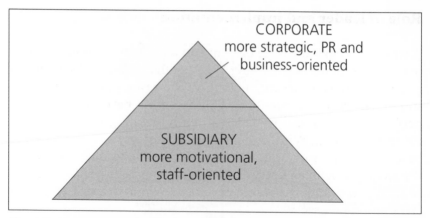

Fig. 1.5: Corporate and subsidiary missions

Corporate mission statements tend to have a more PR role, whereas subsidiary statements need to be more motivational.

WHY HAVE A STRATEGY?

Communication

The strategy is a form of communication that allows people to share and achieve common goals and objectives. Unity and team commitment should result from a strategy that builds on a common set of values and beliefs.

Scarce resources

Strategy also ensures that these goals are achieved through optimal use of resources, such as financial, physical and human, that are generally treated as being quite scarce.

Prioritisation

Rarely can all goals and objectives be fully achieved. Therefore, the strategy has to prioritise the issues and achieve some form of compromise for all stakeholders. Organisations need to ensure the basic values and beliefs of the stakeholders are not compromised, as this will seriously jeopardise the implementation of the strategy.

Role of leader and implementation

A strategy is vital to ensure everyone in an organisation has a frame of reference for decision making. Whether the strategy will be fulfilled in its entirety is irrelevant, as long as the assumptions behind the strategy are clearly understood . This provides a basis for monitoring performance and also provides an early warning mechanism for altering direction. With no strategy, an organisation will lack the basis for comparison and as such will take random decisions that will usually lack timeliness and, maybe, appropriateness. A successful strategy can be defined as one which takes appropriate decisions at an appropriate time.

The future of an organisation is like a thousand mile journey, and the strategy is the first and on-going step! Without the first step there is little direction and, more importantly, little motivation to complete the long and arduous road. It is important to remember that there is always motivation, if the goals are right.

Dynamic world environment

Acting in an appropriate timeframe is critical in today's dynamic and ever changing environment. The only certainty is that tomorrow will be different from today. Emotional detachment from a strategy is critical for success in this dynamic environment.

Strategy needs to be thought of in terms of the past, present and future. *See Fig. 1.6.*

WHO IS RESPONSIBLE FOR CREATING STRATEGY?

Strategy is the responsibility of everyone in the organisation. This may be in the form of taking decisions, collecting data and information or making it work. If someone feels they have no input in any of these, then the question has to be asked "why are you here?"

The process of strategy creation needs to involve as many people as possible. However, circumstances may arise in which decisions need to be taken quickly, maybe in a turnaround situation. These decisions

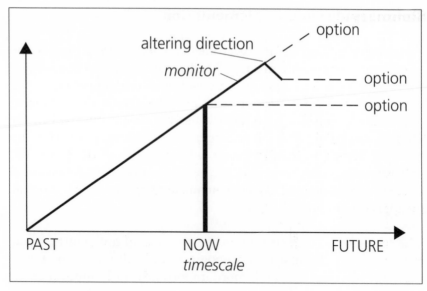

Fig. 1.6: Changing strategies

usually lead to short term results, and as such are well received. However, strategy is, by its very definition, long term. Organisations need to consider the longer term implications of a strategy and thus, where possible, involve as many people from the organisation as possible.

WHEN DO WE THINK ABOUT STRATEGY?

Strategy needs to be considered at all times. It is not sufficient to think about strategy once a year! The strategic process needs to form a major part of the intelligence gathering activity in an organisation. It also needs to be monitored on a continuous and regular basis.

Summary

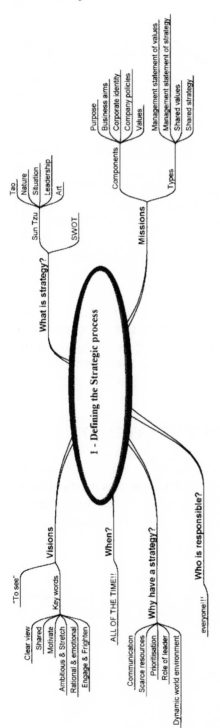

2

STRATEGIC PERSPECTIVES

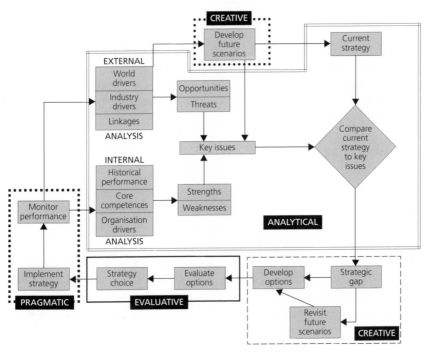

Fig. 2.1: Thinking styles in the Strategic Process

"Creativity is the result of one person seeing another person's perspective."
Unknown

CONCEPTS

The quality of the inputs in a strategic appraisal depends on the variety of perspectives that the organisation can take. There is a tendency to see an organisation from one particular perspective and as a result, it very rarely develops creative solutions to the issues it is facing.

Perspectives are taken through the analysis and it is essential that the analysis is comprehensive and TOTAL. Without a thorough analysis the strategy will possess gaps that, never mind being filled, will actually never be seen, i.e. the water has flowed past an opportunity and the organisation has not noticed it!

Attributes of the strategist

To develop effective and winning strategies requires focus on two particular techniques of thinking which we will now review.

1. Creative Thinking

A major issue in any form of problem solving is the emphasis on identifying solutions. This can be seen through lateral thinking puzzles. The more an individual tries to find a solution, the harder it becomes to think creatively. Consider where Einstein was when he discovered his theories on displacement of water!

The emphasis should be on understanding the situation and all of the assumptions. As our understanding of the situation improves so does the possibility of identifying a creative solution.

To illustrate the above try the following activity:

Activity 1

Cut a cake into eight equal slices with three cuts.

Generally, people will try to identify the solutions. However, if individuals who cannot find a solution study their first attempt, they will see the assumptions they are making about the situation. See *Fig 2.2.* The diagram will highlight to the individual the assumptions being made. Note that without actually drawing what your mind is thinking, it is highly unlikely that the assumptions can be identified. The assumptions that *Fig. 2.2* makes are:

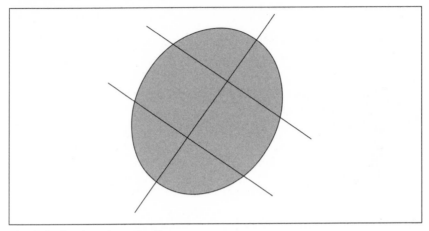

Fig. 2.2: Cutting the cake (i)

- the cake is round
- the cake is two-dimensional

The first assumption, on further inspection, appears to be irrelevant. The second assumption is critical. *Fig. 2.3* shows that once the cake is drawn in three dimensions the solution becomes apparent. As a result of understanding the assumptions we make about a problem, creative solutions become clearer.

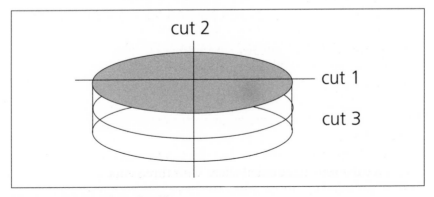

Fig. 2.3: Cutting the cake (ii)

The strategic process ensures that all assumptions are identified so that the creative solutions can be seen. Due to the closeness of individuals to a particular organisation, it becomes very difficult to identify the assumptions being made, because they are so obvious. The analytical mindset that is discussed later is essential to articulating the assumptions.

The restraints to creative thinking are:

- Secondhand thinking – where the strategist takes on another person's view without fully challenging the assumptions behind the view.
- Habit – things are done in a particular way, because they always have been.
- Inferences – a stream of assumptions are made that lead to an incorrect conclusion, e.g. white flakes on ground, therefore it is snowing and therefore very cold.
- Prejudice – judging a situation with emotional content.

Creative thinking skills can be developed by:

- Challenging assumptions
- Teasing out assumptions by continually asking why
- Brainstorming
- Eliminating mindsets
- Gaining a better understanding of the dynamics of the system.

The requirements for strategic thinking, therefore, are:

- An open mind
- Awareness of generalisations, mindsets and mental models (see later)
- Awareness of rationalising prejudices
- Avoidance of personality issues
- Search for evidence, and justifying statements.

An appropriate process for creativity can be as follows:

- Understand the system that the organisation operates in
- Identify all statements – facts, assumptions, prejudices
- Contemplate the problem, without looking for solutions

- Accept frustration
- Relax and switch off from the issue – meditation, change of activity, letting the subconscious work
- Brainstorm ideas and filter inappropriate ideas

2. Systems Thinking

One of the core philosophies that the strategist needs to believe in, to make the strategic process work is the law of cause and effect. This philosophy suggests that every action has a knock on effect at some point in the future. The action may not manifest itself in the most apparent way, but in some other form. Consequently, organisations tend to feel more comfortable addressing symptoms, rather than the true drivers that were responsible in the first place.

The law of cause and effect then implies that the dynamics of a situation are circular, i.e. they continue to impact on the system over a period of time. A branch of thinking has developed called systems thinking which forces the thinker to model the dynamics of any situation, allowing changes to be introduced and tested.

Taking the above into account leads us to consider the strategic process as something that needs to be considered TOTALLY and holistically. The system comprises the external and internal environment which interact with each other in a seamless way. There is little point in building a strategy that focuses entirely on either an external or an internal perspective, as many of the key drivers will be bypassed, leading to ineffective strategies. Building a strategy without focusing at each stage of the process, in its entirety, will lead to incomplete solutions.

The important point at this stage is to ensure that, when carrying out the strategic process, the drivers are constantly sought and challenged for verification. This means that the focus is on asking questions:

who?
what?
why?
where?
when?
how?

This process is followed until the strategist is happy that the true driver is actually found. The strategist is also searching for connections between variables and understanding the impact of relationships between each of the variables over a period of time. Mentally, the skill a strategist needs to develop is the ability to see a number of variables interlinking over time. This is very difficult to do when you consider the breadth of variables an organisation may be dealing with. Therefore, one of the important skills is the ability to prioritise.

As individuals, we may not be able to cope with a complex system comprising hundreds of variables, but we can manage with half a dozen or so. This means that prioritisation of the issues is vital. Software is also available for organisations to model complex systems as a group, and test their assumptions about the business. However, it is recommended that individuals are able to think systemically first before moving on to using software, as the old adage "garbage in, garbage out" has never been more appropriate.

Principles of systems thinking

The area of systems thinking is highly detailed and complex. However, the following is a short step-by-step guide to using the process in a strategic sense.

Step 1 – Define the issue

Broadly define the issue to be solved, but be careful not to home in on solutions – be broad. Be aware that issues occur as a result of the different perspectives that are possible. Therefore, to help define the issue take into account the following elements in your issue definition:

C – Customers – The customer is the group of people getting benefit from the finished product/service.
A – Actors – Actors are the key players participating in the transformation process.
T – Transformation – This is the process of changing an input into a desired output.
O – Owners – The people gaining financial benefit from the transformation.
E – Environment – The external and internal aspects of the organisation.

Step 2 – Brainstorm the variables affecting the system

Brainstorm the variables from the issue definition. This is best achieved using the strategic process for strategy-based issues. List the variables in terms that can be measurable.

Step 3 – Identify the linkages between the variables and to what extent they are dependent on each other

Step 4 – Model the system

The key is to ask the right question, not to find the right answer to the wrong question.

Activity 2

Using systems thinking, identify possible solutions to address the following issue:

> *"As a training manager for a small diversified company, I have identified a resistance to, and neglect of, personal development of line personnel. They cite lack of time and ineffective training as their reasons for this apathy. However, one of the primary objectives of the company is to create a learning culture."*

Mental models

Mental models are internal images we all hold, based on our past experiences. These mental models maybe restrictive in our quest for creativity, and may also inhibit our ability to generate different perspectives. They may blind us to the discontinuities in the dynamic environment. In addition, they can also represent stumbling blocks to the successful implementation of strategy.

Mental models can be overcome by recognising leaps of abstraction, to making generalisations, without challenging our assumptions and testing the basis for our decisions. Overcoming mental models is essential for the development and implementation of creative strategies.

Mindsets and the strategic process

At different stages of the strategic process, the organisation needs to employ appropriate mindsets that maximise the benefits of the exercise.

See *Fig. 2.1* at the beginning of the chapter.

The analytical mindset

Thoroughness in the collection of data, with no preconceptions of the outcome, is vital. The aim of the analyst is to explore the data and trends from various angles and explain particular behaviours. A systemic approach and attention to the fact that the dynamics of the organisation, and its environment, are highly complex needs to be remembered.

The analytical mindset needs to ensure that drivers are found and attention is not given solely to symptoms. Addressing symptoms very rarely yields long term sustainable change – in fact it may well reinforce the problems as the organisation loses sight of the true issues. Addressing the drivers will, without doubt, take longer but will ensure longer term benefits.

Analysis relies heavily on quantitative content, rather than qualitative. Subjectivity needs to be limited, if not eliminated, as this forces the strategists to focus on symptoms, as opposed to the drivers.

Key elements of the analytical mindset are:

- Numeracy
- Questioning
- Rigor
- Attention to detail
- Recognition of anomalies
- "Ivory tower" approach.

The creative mindset

The creative mindset relies on an "everything is possible" attitude. People with experience of a wide variety of industries and life experiences generally provide greater input into the creative part of the strategic process. There is a great need in today's competitive environment for organisations to out-think and out-smart their competition. This suggests they need to challenge the basic rules and accept that everything is possible. A positive attitude is essential. Competitors with good strategists will be trying to "guess" your business's next moves, and as such the possibility of predictability needs to be carefully managed. An organisation might want to be predictable to out-fox the competition.

The key elements of the creative mindset are:

- Positive attitude
- Broad experience
- "Everything is possible" attitude.

The evaluative mindset

Critical to success is the ability to decide, in a thorough manner which direction to take. The evaluative mindset is the balancing view from the creative mindset, or "devil's advocate". This does not mean that this input is negative, but more that it is rigorous in exploring the downsides and upsides of the possibilities.

The key elements of the evaluative mindset:

- open to opposing views
- emotionally detached to the business.

The pragmatic mindset

This mindset is one of the key attributes of an effective leader. This mindset ensures that ideas and strategies are implemented in an effective and efficient manner, as close to design as is possible. The pragmatic mindset also fully accepts that the strategy is an art and not a science, and therefore may need to be changed if obstacles are placed in the way. Some of the key skills of the pragmatist are project management skills, where the leader is totally goal and target driven, with clearly defined timescales and responsibilities.

The key elements of the pragmatic mindset are:

- project management skills
- leadership qualities
- delegative skills
- goal orientation.

Possible solution to Activity 2

Step1 – Define the issue

Customers: Line personnel
Actors: Trainers, both internal and external
Transformation: Application of newly acquired skills through training to facilitate learning
Owners: Company
Environment: Rapidly changing, dynamic environment.

Therefore, the definition is:

> *"Encouraging line personnel to develop, from a personal and business perspective, by using experienced facilitators to benefit organisation learning, and hence, improve business performance in a rapidly changing dynamic environment."*

Step 2 – Brainstorm the variables affecting the system

a Strategic objectives
b Skills levels
c Training programmes
d Applications.

Steps 3 and 4

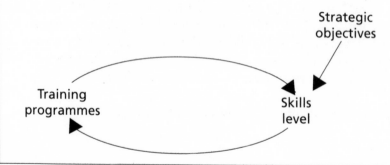

---

which is reflected in the following behaviour over time.

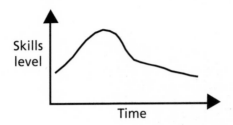

A possible solution to this system would be to include applications as part of the system.

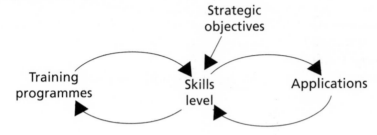

leading to the following behaviour:

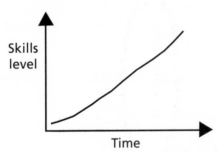

Solutions

- Introduce specific programmes geared to applications.
- Applications linked to strategic objectives.
- Skills level set within objectives.

Summary

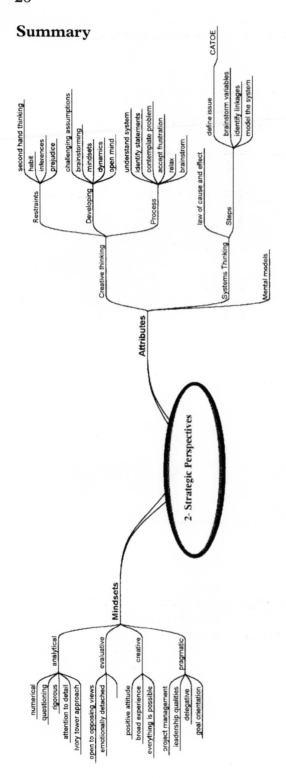

Section B

....

UNDERSTANDING THE EXTERNAL OPPORTUNTIES AND THREATS

3

Analysing the World Drivers of Change

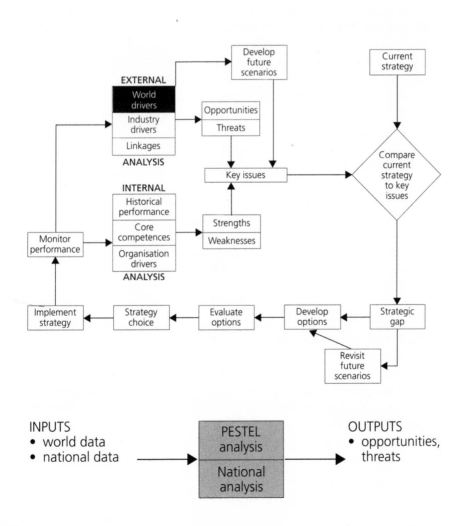

INPUTS
• world data
• national data

PESTEL analysis

National analysis

OUTPUTS
• opportunities, threats

Those who triumph, compute at their headquarters, a
great number of factors, prior to a challenge.
Sun Tzu

CONCEPTS

Analysing drivers

Before looking at the key components of the external analysis, the
purpose of carrying out the analysis needs to be fully understood.
Many analysts explore these drivers as a means of describing the
situation, but take little notice of the outputs in terms of the
development of the strategy. The analysis can yield a substantial
understanding of elements of the future and the likely impact of the
drivers on an organisation. To reach this position, trends need to be
established and understood. Snapshots of a particular driver are fairly
meaningless. Historical data can be used to determine patterns and,
more importantly, the key influencers of these patterns, thus helping
to anticipate future changes in the environment.

The analyst needs, first, to establish whether changes in the
environment are:

- Random fluctuations, i.e. the environmental drivers are
  likely to return to their original state, or

- Permanent changes, i.e. they do not return to their original
  state and there is a fundamental change in the rules of
  competition.

This assessment can help establish the relevance of environmental
changes and drivers to a particular organisation.

The first type of pattern to consider is turning points (ref. 3.1).
These are basic changes in the performance of a variable. The analyst
needs to determine and understand the "stimuli" of the turning
points. What actually is the primary cause of the turning point? There
are many stimuli that may change the rules of the game including
innovation, deregulation and management drivers. The performance

ref. 3.1: Strebel, P., "Breakpoints", (HBS Press, 1992)

of the variable needs to be plotted and the stimuli driving the turning point identified.

Associated with the stimuli are limits to a particular trend. The question needs to be posed, "at what point will this trend stop?" The assumption needs to be made that nothing will continue forever and that at some point a reversal will occur. These limits occur due to some of the following reasons:

- natural laws of science
- market saturation
- negative feedback
- lack of innovation.

Many businesses view their activity with either a pessimistic or an optimistic viewpoint. Very few are able to take a balanced perspective. By assuming nothing continues forever, a more balanced view is possible.

Patterns can also take the form of cycles. Again, this is very similar to the turning points in that the key is to take extreme opposites. Cyclical behaviour can be seen in technological innovation, political factors, social and economic factors. Examples of opposites might be as follows:

- Political – dictatorial v. democratic, left wing v. right wing
- Social – group v. individual behaviour.

Economic cycles can be determined as either short term or long term cycles. Cycles that occur with regular frequency can be used to help determine the timing of future downturns. An example of this is the 50 year economic cycles, known as Kondratiev cycles.

One of the key roles of analysing the external drivers is the recognition of the patterns, by taking into account sufficient history to allow greater appreciation of the key influencers of the business. This approach needs to be applied to all aspects of the analysis.

Determining the drivers

The first stage of the strategic analysis needs to explore the drivers of change that are likely to impact on the strategies of a particular business. These drivers are usually outside the control of most businesses. However, some of the larger, global organisations create advantage by being able to influence these drivers.

These world drivers are, by their very nature, at a level that will affect all businesses and represent the whole system of an organisation. This system needs to be taken into account when analysing the strategy of a company. However, it is very unlikely that any company will be able to take into account all of the drivers. Therefore, it is imperative that companies and their strategists are able to prioritise the factors, working on the Pareto effect, i.e. if a company can address 20% of the drivers, it will probably take account of 80% of the issues it is likely to face in the future.

A question often posed concerns the relevance of carrying out a historical analysis in today's dynamic business environment, where the only guarantee is that tomorrow is totally different from today. This may be the case, but understanding why the business has followed certain patterns and cycles will help improve the quality of strategic decision making, allowing the firm to anticipate, and in some cases initiate, changes to the advantage of the organisation.

The mindset required to maximise the benefit of this analysis is one which takes into account the broadest boundaries of the business activities of the organisation. This will ensure that the organisation is aware of all the opportunities and threats it is able to take account of in its strategy.

During the initial stages of this analysis a broad selection of participants from the stakeholder group needs to be consulted to maximise the benefits of this analysis.

An appropriate acronym used to act as an idea generator for this type of analysis is PESTEL *(see Fig. 3.1)*.

P – Political
E – Economic
S – Social
T – Technological
E – Environment
L – Legal

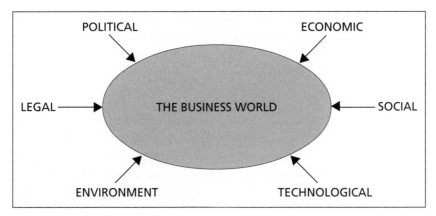

Fig. 3.1: World drivers of change

Political drivers

Political drivers reflect the governmental influences on the business environment and how these are likely to cascade to individual organisations. An organisation needs to consider these influences in relation to all of the key environments and markets the company operates in.

Political drivers manifest themselves in terms of policies and regulations. The political environment also covers the influences of the European Union and other regional trading blocs. These factors affect not only companies operating in Europe, but also companies dealing with European markets. Standardisation is being sought within the world's trading blocs. Some examples of political drivers are:

- Deregulation Acts
- Collapse of communism
- Government Protectionism
- Privatisation
- Opening up of Eastern Europe

Economic drivers

Economic drivers are elements of the economy that impact on the organisation and its markets. These factors largely drive consumer behaviour, as well as the various parts of the business system *(see Fig. 3.2)*. The economic drivers impact on all organisations operating in a particular environment.

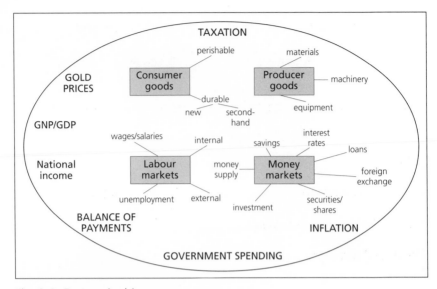

Fig. 3.2: Economic drivers

Social drivers

Social behaviour and attitudes are influenced by many drivers. These are likely to impact on the workforce, and on the consumer. Many different factors need to be monitored and observed for strategic purposes. These are shown in *Fig. 3.3*.

Technological drivers

Many businesses are driven by the rapid changes and advances in technology, thus changing the basis for competition in those businesses. When assessing the drivers the key question to ask is "what advances in technology are driving change in your industry?" These technological advances need to be very specific to truly assess the impact on the business.

Consider the changes, historically, in technology that have changed the nature of the industry. Some examples include:

- Internet/intranet
- Digital technology
- Silicon chip

The impact on technology needs to be considered in terms of the following matrix – *Fig. 3.4.*

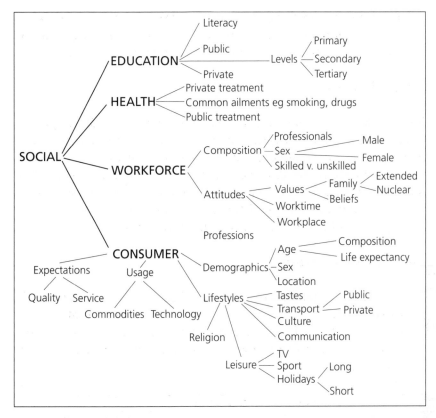

Fig. 3.3: Social drivers

	Key changes	Advances in technology responsible for changes
Process		
Product		
People		
Communication		
Information		

Fig. 3.4: Technology drivers

Environment drivers

The business world has seen a huge increase in interest with regard to environmental issues such as the "Green Effect". As populations become more environmentally aware and conscious of their responsibility to preserve the world environment, companies are increasingly forced to take this into account in their strategies. Some of these issues may manifest themselves under social issues.

Legal drivers

Regulatory and legal factors are those drivers that shape the framework of industries, the environments and markets in which they operate. These factors are probably the easiest to monitor as they are likely to be enforced. However, organisations need to understand the dynamics of regulation and the legal process, aligned with the political motives of the environment, so as to be able to anticipate regulations that are to come into being.

Issue Prioritisation

The Influence/Impact matrix is a useful tool to assist the analyst in prioritising the drivers identified in the PESTEL analysis and subsequent analyses. However, if the drivers are vague and not clearly defined, then the prioritisation process becomes significantly more difficult *see Fig. 3.5.*

Driver	Influence on industry (0 to 10)	Impact on company (-5 to +5)	(A) x (B)	Notes
	(A)	(B)		

Fig. 3.5: Influence/impact matrix

KEY POINTS

- Ensure the factors are broad and cover all elements of the company's business environment.
- Ensure the factors are specific and clearly tangible.
- Priority is to identify the factors, not necessarily to place them in the right category.

Activity 3

Identify the key external drivers affecting your business.

National Advantage

There are many organisations able to gain advantage from the position of the nation in which it operates. Porter, (ref. 3.2) states that governments and nations can help create advantage for a company by strategically looking at its National Diamond. The elements of the National Diamond are shown in *Fig. 3.6*.

The four key determinants are:

1. Firm Strategy, Structure and Rivalry
Firms tend to have a common approach to strategy, structure and competition, which makes the transfer of employees from one environment to another much easier. Companies from some nations share common beliefs in terms of strategy, in terms of the way the business is structured and the basis on which it competes. For example, Swiss companies generally compete on the basis of differentiation.

2. Factor Conditions
Elements of the market, whether it be the employment or consumer market, create a unique advantage for organisations from these markets. Switzerland is a good example of a nation that has used its unique environment to create advantage for its local companies. Education is an area that the Swiss government has invested in heavily to create leverage in the employment market. Porter terms this a Factor Creation Mechanism.

ref. 3.2: Porter, M., "Competitive Advantage of Nations", (The Free Press, 1990)

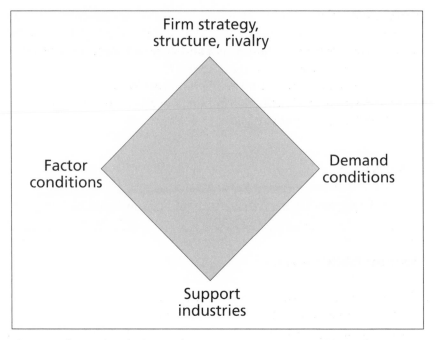

Fig. 3.6: The National Diamond. Source: Porter, "Competitive Advantage of Nations", The Free Press, 1990.

3. Demand Conditions

Conditions of the marketplace and demand create pressures to which companies need to respond. This may be the size of market or the demands of the market. Porter cited the example of Switzerland where the market is very demanding and seeks high quality, thus forcing its companies to deliver high quality, usually in the high cost, niche markets.

4. Support Industries

A network may exist in a particular market where a multitude of industries "assist" each other to create a unique advantage. An example of this is the French airport sector, where the French airport companies have created a consulting sector to compete on the international airport market, with the sole intention of winning contracts to benefit French suppliers. This approach is heavily supported and encouraged by the government, particularly as the French airports are government owned.

Each of the above is a potential opportunity or threat for any firm within that environment. Organisations need to explore whether there is a source of advantage to be gained and how this may be exploited.

Singapore and Dubai are excellent examples of nations that have created a unique advantage for their national companies in the international environment, by controlling and leading business policy.

This analysis needs to be taken into account in terms of the home nation, the market nation and any partner nations, so as to establish the possible threats and, more importantly, the opportunities that may face the organisation. Careful analysis will allow the organisation to cover itself in terms of its strategic approach.

Fig. 3.7 shows the format for analysis.

CATEGORY	Low	Med-ium	High	0 Threats	10 Opportunities	Comments
FIRM STRUCTURE, STRATEGY, RIVALRY						
Types of rivalry: • cost leadership • Differentiation • Focus • Service-oriented • Competitor driven • Process driven • Innovative						
Structure: • Matrix • Functional • Divisional • Process • Transnational • Global • Multinational						
Attitude to: competition • co-operate • compete						
FACTOR: • Uniqueness of market • Factor creation mechanisms						
DEMAND: • market size compared to other markets • cost focus • quality focus • time sensitive • service sensitive						
SUPPORT: • Breadth of industries						

Fig. 3.7: National Diamond analysis

Solution to Activity 3

The following is a list of external drivers affecting the tele-communications industry in the UK. Impact is considered for a company like BT.

Political:
- Regulatory intervention
- Liberalisation of telecoms earlier than the majority of other countries.

Economic:
- Accounting rate bypass mechanism. This is the method of payment between international operators for terminating calls
- Adverse currency fluctuations.

Social:
- Increase in use of the Internet
- Premium rate services.

Technological:
- Intelligent network platform. This allows different services to be offered.

Factor	Influence on industry (0 to 10)	Impact on company (+5 to -5)	Score
Regulatory intervention	9	-4	-36
Liberalisation	10	+4	+40
Accounting rate bypass	8	+3	+24
Adverse currency fluctuations	7	-1	-7
Increase in use of Internet	5	+1	+5
Premium rate services	6	+2	+12

Fig. 3.5a: Activity 3 solution

Activity 4

Construct the National Diamond for Switzerland.

Solution to Activity 4

Firm strategy, structure and rivalry:
- International companies
- Strategies based on differentiation
- Highly differentiated.

Demand conditions:
- Small domestic market, therefore need to be more international
- Geography
- Affluent market – high value items
- Multiple cultures.

Factor conditions:
- Education – a factor creation mechanism
- Few natural resources – bank secrecy laws
- Political neutrality – good infrastructure
- Four languages – location.

Support industries:
- Broad base of industries.

Analytical steps

1. Carry out a PESTEL analysis
a. Brainstorm all factors with a representative group of stakeholders
b. Collect data to determine trends
c. Justify key points and discuss with team
d. Plot the trends and cycles for the key variables
e. Determine the patterns and test the stimuli and limits

2. Carry out the National Diamond analysis
a. Define the nation to be analysed
b. Interview local experts with market knowledge
c. Gather data from government sources
d. Complete National Diamond matrix, *Fig. 3.7*
e. Identify the key points, opportunities and threats

3. Produce a list of all of the issues in the table *Fig 3.5*

4. Identify the key issues by prioritising the list

5. Determine the opportunities and threats

Summary

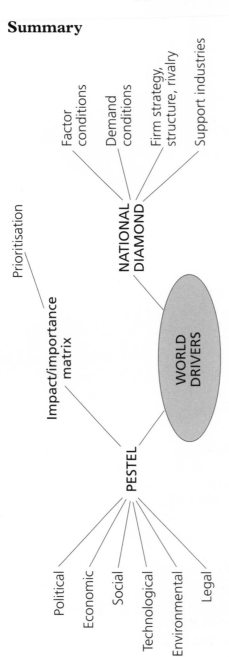

4

ANALYSING THE INDUSTRY

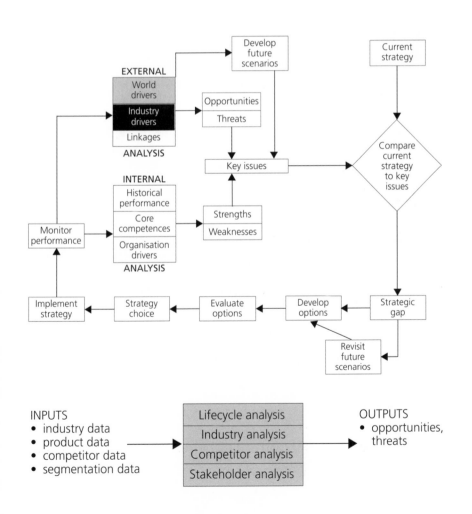

"Make the best quality of goods at the lowest cost,
paying the highest wages possible."
Henry T. Ford

CONCEPTS

The first stage of industry analysis involves defining the industry.
This definition needs to be very specific and tangible. The definition
should focus on the benefits that the business is actually attempting
to deliver to its customer base. During the initial stages a broader
definition is encouraged so as to ensure that gaps are not left in the
appraisal.

The industry may be defined in terms of the following:

- product – the tangible output
- process – the primary activities along the chain of events
- target market/segment and geographical scope
- people employed in the organisation
- customer benefits to be delivered
- image to be portrayed

Fig. 4.1 shows a format for defining your business.

Lifecycle analysis

A key part of the analysis is to establish the stage the industry is at
(see Fig. 4.2). Companies can identify the stage of their business by
exploring the characteristics of each stage and comparing these with
their own situation. *Fig. 4.3* shows the typical characteristics of each
of the stages. The key skill of the analyst is to anticipate the oncoming
stage early enough to influence the strategy of the organisation.

The lifecycle analysis is another pattern (see Chapter 3) that we
may want to explore to help in anticipating market changes.

Industry threats

All organisations face potential threats from many different angles
which need to be determined as a key input into the strategy.

Variable	Description
Process	
Product	
Market	
People	
Benefits	
Image	

Fig 4.1: Industry definition

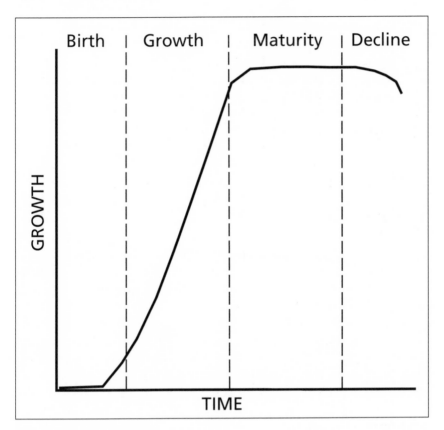

Fig. 4.2: Lifecycle analysis

Industry characteristic	Birth	Growth	Maturity	Decline
Demand	High income buyers. Buyers need convincing and educating	Rapidly increasing market penetration.	Mass market, replacement/repeat buying	Customers knowledgeable.
Technology	Not standard technology.	Some technologies eliminated.	Well-diffused technical know-how; quest for technological improvements.	
Products	Poor quality. Wide variety. Frequent design changes.	Design and quality improves. Reliability of key importance.	Standardisation lessens differentiation. Minor model changes predominate.	Product differentiation lessens.
Manufacture and distribution	Short production runs. High skilled labour content. Specialised distribution channels.	Capacity shortages. Mass production. Competition for distribution.	Emergence of over-capacity. Deskilling of protection. Long production runs. carried by distributers.	Heavy over-capacity. Re-emergence of speciality channels.
Trade	Shift of manufacture from advanced countries to poorer countries.			
Competition	Few companies.	Entry with many mergers and failures.	Shake out. Price competition increases.	Price wars, exits.
Key success factors	Product innovation. Support services. Establishing credible image of firm and product.	Design to allow large-scale manufacture. Access to distribution. Establishing strong brand.	Cost-efficiency scale, process innovation, buyer selection.	Reduce overheads. Signal commitment. Rationalise capacity.

Fig. 4.3: Characteristics of life cycle stages

The threats facing an industry is a function of six forces *(see Fig. 4.4)*. These forces also help define the industry on an iterative basis. The analysis is based on research carried out by Michael Porter. Each force influences the state of the industry.

The six forces are:

1. Threat of new entrants

The strength of the threat of the entry depends on:

- barriers to entry that existing competitors have put up, and the
- anticipated reaction from existing competitors.

Factors that contribute to the above are:

Economies of scale – These are lower unit costs that arise from producing at a greater scale of output. Organisations will tend to enter an industry if they can match or better the costs of the current players in a business.

Product differentiation – New players may need to invest heavily to overcome customer loyalty that may have been generated by brand loyalty.

Switching costs – These are the costs that may be incurred in switching from existing players to new players in an industry.

Regulation – Government policy related to areas such as licensing and safety regulation might create obstacles for potential new entrants.

Capital investment – The need to invest large amounts in fixed assets, stocks, customer credit etc. can deter many new entrants.

Working capital requirement – Certain industries suffer from cashflow problems during the early stages of start up.

Access to distribution channels – In the current climate of partnership access to retailers, wholesalers can cause great difficulty for newcomers.

New entrants to an industry have the effect of increasing the capacity and employing strategies that focus on areas such as pricing. However, the question needs to be raised for existing players, "why does this opportunity exist for a new entrant to have an edge?" Many organisations in "comfortable" positions, eg. monopoly or protected

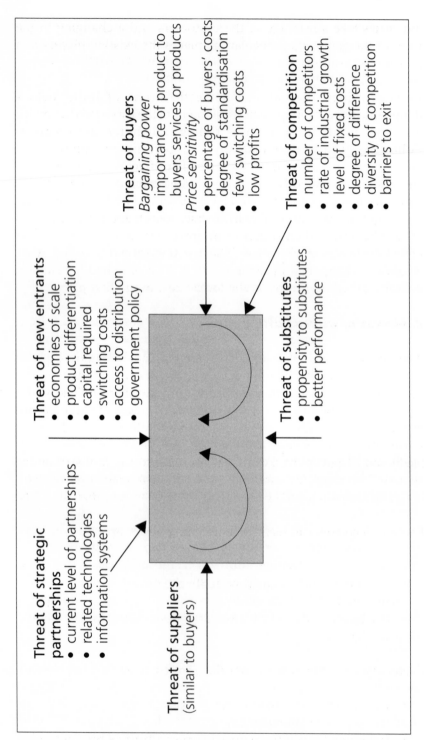

Fig.4.4: Six forces analysis

industries take advantage of the customers and a changing in the rules of the game, eg. deregulation, places the existing players in a precarious position.

Indian Airlines, the national domestic airline of India, held a dominant, in fact monopolistic, position until the early-1990s. Service was poor in all areas, such as timing, reliability and comfort. Following pseudo liberalisation (the government allowed the introduction of air taxi operations, which in effect became very large air taxis that operated B737s!) new airlines entered the market with strategies focusing on improved levels of service and better pricing. Overnight, Indian Airlines' market share went from nearly 100% to 75%. The airline then began to improve service to compete, and halted the loss in market share. The question should be asked, what would have happened in the industry if the airline had focused on delivering the best service at the lowest cost in the first place?

2. Threat of buyers and suppliers

The threat of buyers and suppliers is a function of bargaining power and price sensitivity. The bargaining power is determined by the number of buyers and their respective market shares. Clearly, the fewer the number of buyers the greater the power of these buyers over a particular industry. The threat is also influenced by the price sensitivity of the buyers. Consideration needs to be given to the likelihood of buyers backward integrating into the industry under analysis. This threat increases if the proportion of cost to total revenue is significantly high and at the same time little value is being added.

Factors to consider in terms of bargaining power are:

- the number of buyers
- the importance of the product to the buyer's services or products
- the balance of power between the customers/suppliers and the industry.

Factors to consider in terms of price sensitivity are:

- the percentage of total buyers' costs
- the degree of standardisation
- switching costs – these arise because a buyer's product specifications tie in to particular suppliers.

Segmentation analysis
When considering the threat of buyers, it is important to look at the
structure of the industry in terms of the segments that exist and the
needs of the different segments. The segments need to be determined
in terms of the benefits sought by the customer groups.

Data that needs to be analysed include:

- Total population trends
- Segment potential
- Segment trends
- Benefits sought by segment
- Income trends.

Customer analysis
The assessment of loyalty of particular customer groups needs to be
taken into account in objective terms. Objectivity is key as very few
customers are loyal because of an emotional attachment. Generally,
loyalty is tied in to the goals of the customer and thus it is important
to carry out a customer analysis in terms of the variables cited in the
competitor analysis later in this chapter.

3. Threat of substitutes

Customers have the option of getting a similar benefit from associated
industries. For example, if a tour operator considers its industry to
be the provision of foreign holidays, then it will consider its substitutes
to include domestic holidays. However, if the tour operator sees its
industry slightly more broadly, it may see other leisure activities,
such as purchasing entertainment systems, as potential substitutes.

In analysing the threat of substitutes, the propensity to substitute of
the customer base needs to be taken into account. Clearly, this may
be a very dynamic factor based on many other variables, such as
disasters, environmental factors, public perception, etc. The
propensity to substitute depends on the extent to which the customer
can gain greater benefit, in performance, from different industries.

4. Threat of internal strategic partnerships

Consolidation in the industry creates greater concentration in the
industry and as a result can fundamentally change the industry
structure. This is happening to a very significant degree in the United

States in the airline industry. The Big Six, i.e. American, United, Delta, Continental, USAir and Northwest, have created partnerships by joining forces – American/USAir, Delta/Continental, United/ Northwest. These partnerships have changed the basis for competition, and have been largely driven by technology, in the exploitation of Computer Reservation Systems (CRS).

5. *Threat of competition*

The level of threat of direct competition to the industry is a function of the following:

Market size – What is the current size of the market?
Market growth rate – What is the rate of growth of the market and how is it changing?
Number of players – How many players are there and how has this changed historically?
Market shares – What are the market shares of the players being monitored? How have these changed?
Level of fixed costs – What is the level of fixed costs? Can these be overcome, eg. through leasing of plant and machinery, etc? The higher the level of fixed costs, the greater the likelihood that existing players will try to maintain their positions through price cutting. For example, in aircraft manufacturing the level of fixed costs is so high that manufacturers, particularly of smaller regional type aircraft, are prepared to sell the products at ridiculously low prices.
Degree of differentiation – What level of branding and product differentiation exists?
Diversity of competition – What are the core businesses of the competitors? Are they associated with other businesses? What are their key activities and what role does this industry play in their portfolio?
Barriers to exit – How easy is it to get out of the business?

Analysing the competition

> "*If you know your enemy and yourself, you will win every battle.*
> *If you know yourself but not your enemy, for every battle won, you will suffer a loss.*
> *If you are ignorant of both your enemy and yourself you are a fool and certain to be defeated in every battle*" *– Sun Tzu*

A major output of the analysis is to identify who the key players and competitors are within the defined industry. Once the competitors have been identified it is important to ensure information is collected on a regular basis, combining published information with intelligence gathered through the organisation.

In determining the competition to be analysed, the radius of competition needs to be agreed. The radius of competition is essentially the geographical scope of possible competitors. In today's climate, and as we strive towards a global economy with few trade barriers, these competitors could come from anywhere in the world.

The levels of intelligence that need to be considered are strategic and tactical. Strategic information relates to goals and long range plans of the company, including its objectives, whereas tactical intelligence relates to some of the nearer term actions, such as pricing, product development, design, etc.

Typical information you need to compare is as follows:

Strategic level

- Vision
- Mission
- Strategies employed
- Objectives
- Tactics
- Management and leadership styles
- Parent organisation and relationships
- Other affiliations
- Number of employees
- Uses of technology
- Geographical scope
- Core competencies
- Financial performance
- Sales growth
- Growth margin – cost of sales by type/product, mix analysis – expenses/sales
- Operating margin – sales/employee, average pay/employee
- Stock days
- Debtor days
- Creditor days
- Fixed assets/sales

- Acid and current ratios
- Gearing
- Return on capital employed.

In fact, a detailed analysis of the strengths and weaknesses of the companies along the lines of analysis carried out for your own organisation (see Section C) can be followed. Although some of the information may be very difficult to get hold of, this should not deter you from carrying out the analysis.

The ideal spread of information will allow the design of a systematic gathering mechanism which is ultimately owned by everyone in the organisation. Sales people, engineers, accountants will all have access to different people and sources of information. The key is to get everyone sharing the information for the benefit of the organisation as a whole.

Presentation of competitor data, for greatest effect, is crucial. This needs to be creative and meaningful. *Figs 4.5, 4.6* and *4.7* show some examples of presenting data. Be creative and have fun.

Activity 5

Identify the key threats, using Fig. 4.11 for an industry of your choice.

Stakeholder Analysis

The stakeholder represents a fundamental part of any organisation. It represents the organisation's ability to manage the needs and expectations of the group of people most heavily associated with the industry. Certain elements of the stakeholders are external and there are groups that are also internal. We shall include the analysis for both groups in this section.

First, identify the stakeholders. These may include the following:

Internal

- Owners and shareholders
- Employees
- Corporate management.

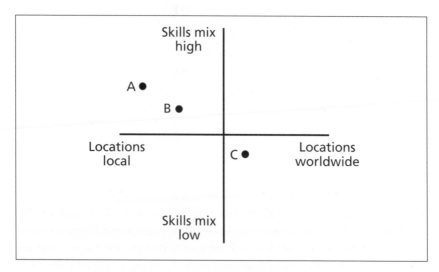

Fig. 4.5: Presenting competitor data, space diagrams

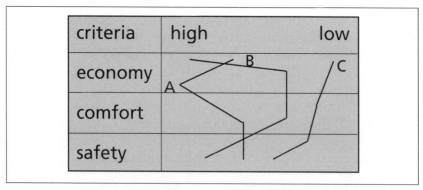

Fig. 4.6: Presenting competitor data, comparison graphs

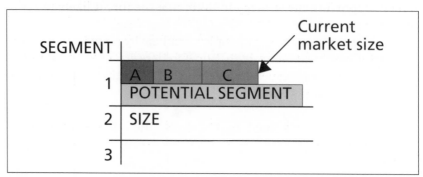

Fig. 4.7: Presenting competitor data, market maps

External

- Creditors
- Customers
- Unions
- Local communities
- Government
- Suppliers
- Competitors
- Public interest groups.

The purpose of the stakeholder analysis is to determine the assumptions different groups make about the industry. Some of these assumptions will support the industry and thus create opportunities, and some will resist, giving rise to threats. Consequently, the analysis needs to be carried out once a strategy has been decided on or is being considered.

For each stakeholder identify the supporting and resisting assumptions and state them on a table *(see Fig. 4.8)*. Assess the importance of the assumption on the strategy and the degree of certainty attached to the assumption. A 0 to 10 scale may be used for both parameters, with 0 representing low importance and low certainty, 10 representing high importance and high certainty. The assumptions can be plotted on a graph – *Fig. 4.9*. The graph can be used to determine the key factors to take into account.

Stating these assumptions will allow the organisation to carry out a forcefield analysis *(see Fig. 4.10)* and determine how best to use the forces supporting the strategy to overcome the forces likely to resist the strategy.

Stakeholders	Major assumptions	Importance	Certainty
A	Supporting		
	Resisting		
B			

Fig. 4.8: Stakeholder assumptions

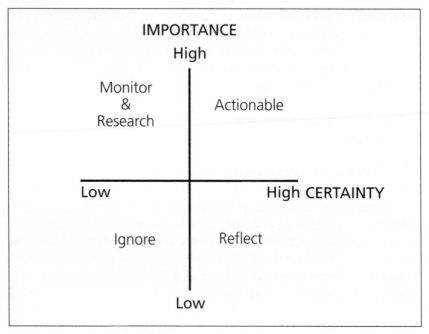

Fig. 4.9: Stakeholder analysis

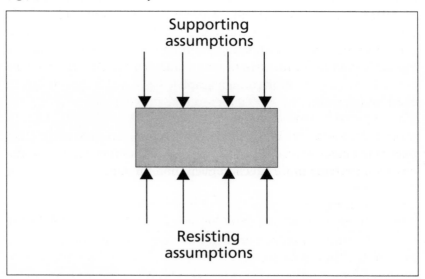

Fig. 4.10: Forcefield analysis

Sample Solution to Activity 5: Private banking industry in Luxembourg

Typical constraints are a client's investment horizon, his degree of risk aversion (normally resulting in an agreement on a portfolio's asset allocation between interest bearing instruments and stocks) and fiscal legislation, (most countries treat capital gains more favourably than income such as dividends or interest earnings, or favour life insurance above other forms of financial investment), including inheritance taxes.

1. Rivalry between existing competitiors (low to average, but increasing).

1.1   Number and balance of competitors.
The existence of some 220 banks (mainly Belgo-Luxembourgeois, German, Swiss and Dutch origin) in a country of 400,000 inhabitants, seems to indicate an intense level of competition. However, this first impression has to be qualified, as the bulk of private banking activity in Luxembourg concentrates on non-residents, who generally prefer to work with subsidiaries of financial institutions from their own country. Over the years, most banks brought their customers with them, instead of competing for existing customers. Nonetheless, competition for upscale European customers is increasing, not only between Luxembourg-based banks or between Luxembourg- and Swiss-based banks, but also between 'domestic' banks on the one hand, and Luxembourg and Swiss banks on the other. The latter phenomenon can also be described as an intensification of competition between onshore and offshore banking.

1.2 Exit barriers.
The required investment to start a bank is not particularly high (it takes a minimum of Euro5m of capital to create a bank, and a large part of the costs are variable (personnel, buildings, etc), so that exit costs are perhaps more psychological than financial.

1.3 Growth rates.
The most important factor for being optimistic about private banking is that it is undoubtedly a growth industry, perhaps the major one outside the high-tech sector. As a result of more than 50 years of peace and prosperity in the OECD countries, the creation of an entrepreneurial class in emerging markets and soaring financial markets, the amount of worldwide financial savings is steadily increasing. Many of those having inherited wealth or wishing to diversify their portfolio turn to banks for professional advice. Moreover, in Europe, upscale clients have frequently found it difficult to find appropriate private banking advice in their own country.

2. The bargaining power of buyers/clients (relatively low, but increasing...)

Pressure on private banking fees is likely to increase as markets are rapidly becoming more transparent and competitive due to the Internet (readily available information, bargain electronic trading) and the introduction of the Euro. Nevertheless, clients are very numerous and even the biggest clients hold no more than a fraction of the total assets managed by (or given in custody to) the banks. Despite some pressure, fee schedules are generally adhered to. There is also a tendency to let customers benefit from IT-derived cost savings while increasing fees for higher value-added services such as discretionary asset management.

It is also worth noting that in private banking non-fee factors play an important role. Clients are often more concerned about excessive (front) staff turnover than about costs. This is to the advantage of the banks which, by managing human resources well, can extract a premium from their clients.

3. The bargaing power of suppliers (weak and weakening...)

External suppliers (mostly foreign banks and brokers) offer crucial services, most notably in the areas relating to securities (execution of orders, custody, clearing), FX (Foreign Exchange) and deposits. They are themselves under unrelenting pressure from their competitors to lower prices and improve service (e.g. the reduction of settlement from Trade +5 to Trade +3). A bank can switch clearer or custodian bank without major costs, and without causing any interruption to its business.

4. The threat of new entrants (low, more theoretical than real)

In theory, the threat of new entrants is very real. As mentioned under (2), minimum capital requirements are fairly low at Euro5m. Moreover, in Europe, private banking is not only the preserve of commercial or universal banks, as non-bank brokers may also operate in this market. Nevertheless, the tendency of clients to stick to well-known, rated banks is a reality, allowing banks to extract a safety premium from their clients. Clients switching to major mutual fund houses are also the exception, probably because fees are very high and customers lack personalised service.

5. The threat of substitute products (low)

As a result of the absence of patent protection and the absence of legal restrictions, most banks within the EU are able to copy and offer any 'product' within a very short time span. Hence innovations benefit only during a short period from exceptional profit margins as new products turn into 'commodities' as soon as they are copied widely. (Think, for example, of the first FX and interest swap between the World Bank and IBM more than ten years ago. Within months, every financial institution throughout the OECD had the possibility to use this product or to offer it to its clients.) Moreover, the EU's adoption of universal banking means that roughly any financial service can be offered by banks or *ad hoc* subsidiaries, including insurance products.

Conclusion

Private banking is a market of the future. While competition will intensify, the position of banks is bound to strengthen over the medium term.

Analytical Steps

1 Collect data on the six forces
2 Complete analysis of forces *(Fig. 4.11)*
3 Determine and prioritise the threats posed by the industry
4 Carry out the competitor analysis
5 Identify the external shareholders and their assumptions
6 Determine the opportunities and threats

Factor	Low 0 1 2 3 / Level 4 5 6 7 8 9 / High 10	Justification
1. Industry definition		
2. Threat of new entrants due to:		
• economies of scale		
• product differentiation		
• switching costs		
• regulation		
• capital investment		
• working capital requirement		
• access to distribution channels		
3. Threat of buyers due to:		
• number of buyers		
• importance of product to buyers services		
• power of buyers		
• proportion of buyers' cost		
• degree of standardisation		
• switching costs		
• customer loyalty		
4. Threat of suppliers due to:		
• number of suppliers		
• importance of product to suppliers services		
• power of suppliers		
• proportion of suppliers' cost		
• degree of standardisation		
• switching costs		
5. Threat of substitutes due to:		
• propensity to substitute		
6. Threat of competition due to:		
• market size		
• market growth rate		
• number of players		
• market shares		
• level of fixed costs		
• degree of differentiation		
• diversity of competition		
• barriers to exit		
7. Threat of internal strategic partnership due to:		
• concentration trends		
• dependence on technology		
• linkage in information systems		

Fig. 4.11: Industry analysis

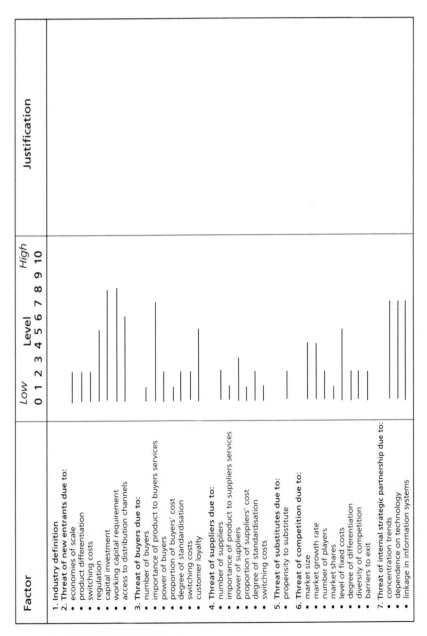

Fig. 4.11a: Activity 5 solution

Summary

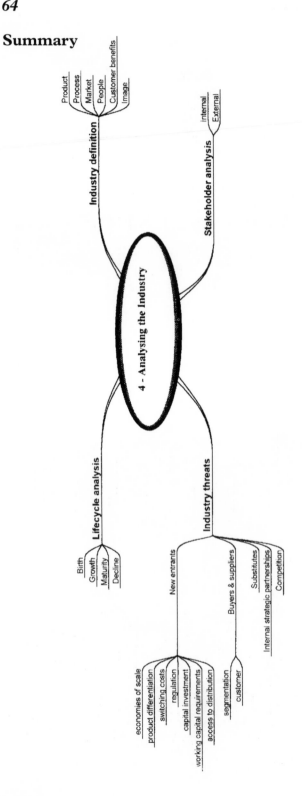

5

DETERMINING THE LINKAGES BETWEEN INDUSTRIES

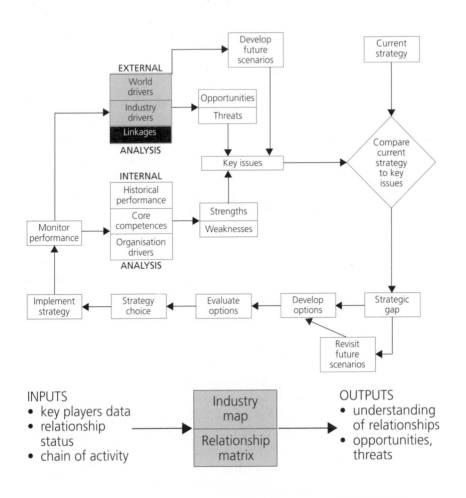

INPUTS
- key players data
- relationship status
- chain of activity

Industry map

Relationship matrix

OUTPUTS
- understanding of relationships
- opportunities, threats

"Decide what you want.
Decide what you are willing to exchange for it.
Establish your priorities.
Go to work"
H.L. Hunt, Oil Executive

CONCEPTS

Each and every industry is connected with a variety of other
industries, either as suppliers or buyers. The relationships, by their
very nature, leave organisations open to threats in terms of
competition and the potential entry of these buyers and suppliers
into a particular industry. It is important for all industries to
understand the nature of these relationships and so increase their
awareness of potential opportunities and threats. Indeed, some
organisations actually create strategies around these relationships.
This is due to the fact that if managed properly these relationships
can yield huge advantages for the organisation, either in terms of
reduced costs or increased business opportunities.

Within a strategic framework it is important to analyse the nature of
relationships, not only for your own organisation, but also for your
key competitors. In fact, the perspective to be taken is of the industry
as a whole. This analysis will explore all other industries connected
in any way, and show the nature of relationships. There are differing
degrees of relationship varying from a simple supplier-buyer
relationship to equity based relationships.

The aim of the analysis is to identify potential opportunities and
threats. Good diagramming techniques are key to a worthwhile
analysis. Considerable information can be contained in a simple
diagram which allows the analyst to identify possible sources of
strategic advantage.

In an ideal world all organisations would strive to carry out all
activities, including those as supplier and buyer, within their
boundaries. This ensures maximum control in terms of cost and
quality of service. Benefits for the consumer, or end customer, lie in
the fact that they should receive maximum value added for minimal
cost, in a consistent manner, with one organisation maintaining full
accountability of all aspects of the service. However, this would incur
a huge cost, with the organisation not necessarily focusing on its

unique advantages and competencies. Therefore, organisations explore the possibility of creating links, whether formal or informal, with related companies which possess unique advantages and competencies through their specialisation.

In reality, there are many downsides to "contracting out" these related activities. These include:

- lack of commitment to schedules
- lack of quality control
- poor accountability
- lack of meeting design specification

To ensure an organisation can truly gain benefit from outsourcing activities, it needs to create competencies in managing relationships between organisations in different industries. In addition, the systems and reporting mechanisms need to be in place to tie in with the overall strategy of the organisation. This ensures that focus is maintained on the critical success factors of the business.

Many organisations try to create advantage by protecting themselves from the onset of any threats from suppliers and buyers through the nature of the relationship. Examples include companies like Ford and Marks & Spencer. These companies will deliberately seek smaller suppliers, with insufficient power to impose themselves on the industry in any major way. However, the downside of this approach is that these companies are relying on their presence and size to create advantage, and therefore it is not based on trust and "win-win" for all players. Some companies, like the US discount retailer Wal-Mart, build their position around working with their suppliers to create win-win situations, and thus sharing strategy to a certain extent.

The areas in which organisations should endeavour to create advantage through their linkages include:

- **conformance** to design specifications.
- **performance** – ensuring the grade of service or product is of an adequate level that meets with the strategic objectives of the organisation. Customers are usually prepared to pay more for better performance.
- **quick response** – usually measured in terms of delays or elapsed time.

- **reliability** – can be described as a failure free operation over a period of time.
- **humanity** – providing service or goods with the right degree of friendliness, attentiveness, humility and honesty.

The analysis needs to explore:

- how the organisation can develop relationships
- which organisations in the system best fulfil the above criteria
- which relationships have potential gaps in the above criteria
- the degree to which the organisation successfully manages relationships

The relationship matrix, *Fig. 5.1,* allows the analysis of relationships in a tabular format which can then be used for constructing the Industry map *(Fig 5.2)*. Use the relationship matrix to classify the perceived value of a linkage. A blank box assumes that a relationship exists but there is little cohesion in the delivery of the key criteria. A shaded box indicates that it works to some extent, but still has a long way to go in terms of fulfilling its potential. A fully coloured box indicates the relationship works well and will be difficult to break down.

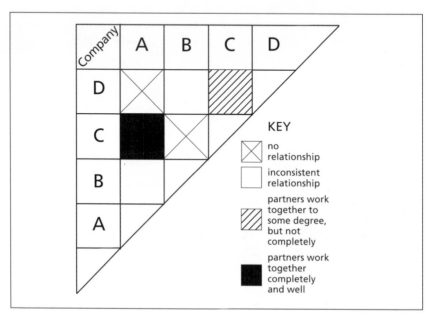

Fig. 5.1: Relationship matrix

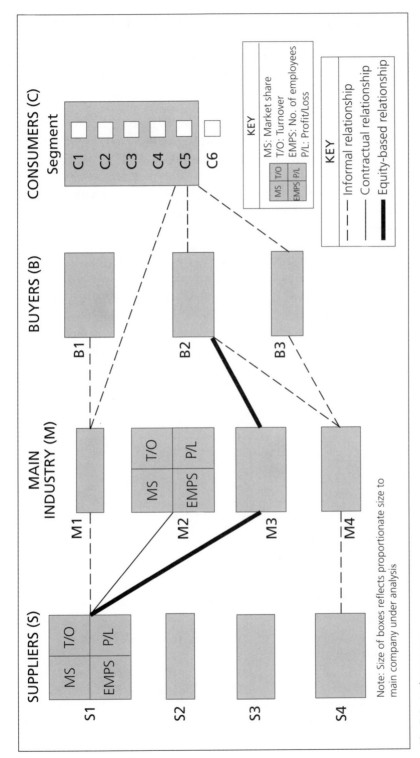

Fig 5.2: Industry map

Completing the relationship matrix will be largely a subjective exercise, but should be based on data collected from interviews with suppliers, buyers and possibly competitors. Customers should be interviewed to understand where organisations are failing to deliver maximum value. Data collected may be indirect, based on informal discussions between company staff and other organisations' staff. The analysis will identify a breakdown in elements of the chain which may be exploited by competitors. Equally, the analysis may show that the relationship is working reasonably well. The questionnaire should be incorporated into the overall competitor analysis.

Activity 6

Construct the industry map for an industry of your choice, and show the relationships.

Solution to Activity 6: eg Low-cost airlines

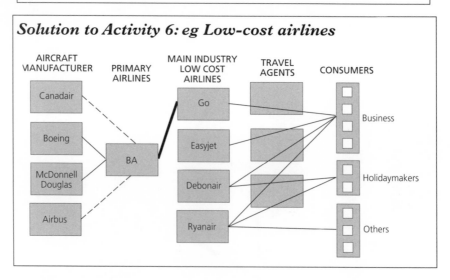

Analytical steps

1 Draw the chain of activities of your business in process format
2 Gather data on size of companies in terms of revenue, market share and employees
3 Take either the size of your own company or the largest one and assume that this will be the datum size of the boxes to be used in the diagram
4 Construct all other boxes relative to the size of the datum box

5 Collect data from publications, talking to other players etc. in terms of the nature of relationships
6 Complete industry map
7 Construct relationship matrix
8 Place the names of all players in columns and rows
9 Construct the diagram as shown
10 Identify opportunities and threats
 - List the key issues arising from analysis
 - Include in *Fig. 4.11*
 - List opportunities and threats.

Summary

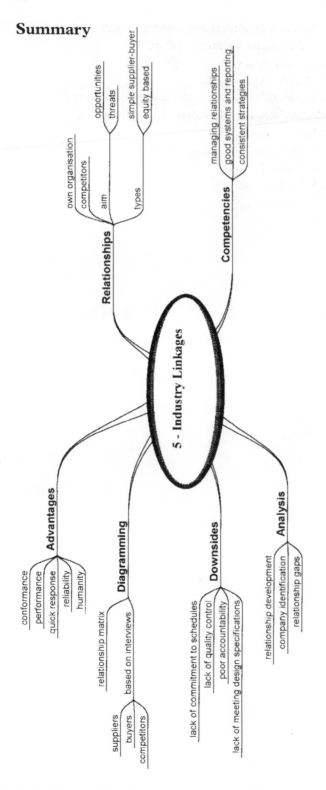

Relationships
- aim
  - own organisation
  - competitors
  - opportunities
  - threats
- types
  - simple supplier-buyer
  - equity based

Competencies
- managing relationships
- good systems and reporting
- consistent strategies

Advantages
- conformance
- performance
- quick response
- reliability
- humanity

Diagramming
- relationship matrix
- based on interviews
  - suppliers
  - buyers
  - competitors

Downsides
- lack of commitment to schedules
- lack of quality control
- poor accountability
- lack of meeting design specifications

Analysis
- relationship development
- company identification
- relationship gaps

5 - Industry Linkages

Section C

. . . .

**UNDERSTANDING THE
INTERNAL STRENGTHS
AND WEAKNESSES**

6

HISTORICAL PERFORMANCE

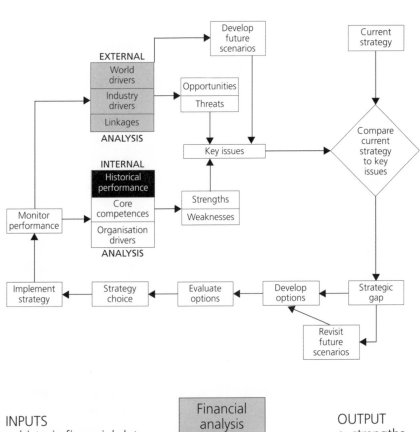

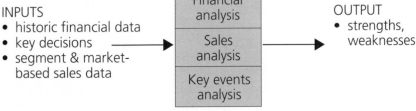

INPUTS
- historic financial data
- key decisions
- segment & market-based sales data

Financial analysis

Sales analysis

Key events analysis

OUTPUT
- strengths, weaknesses

"To lift an autumn leaf is not an act of great strength,
To see the sun and moon is not an act of sharp sight,
To hear a sudden thunderclap is not an act of acute
listening."
Sun Tzu

CONCEPTS

Why analyse historical performance?

Historical analysis of internal company and external environment data develops an understanding of the relationships between the external environment, key strategic decisions and the performance of the organisation *(Fig. 6.1)*. Any worthwhile analysis needs to explore the reasons and causes of the levels of performance being achieved. Key strengths and weaknesses of the results of the analysis need to be pulled out, so that they may be incorporated in any new strategy.

The historical data also shows the time lags between key events and their impact on the performance of the organisation. This enables the analyst to appreciate the dynamics of the organisation and its environment. Historical analysis provides an indication as to the effectiveness of the management of an organisation, thus identifying potential strengths and weaknesses of the management team.

The analysis of the historical performance of the organisation needs to be linked with the results of the various external analyses to improve understanding of the dynamics of the business.

Scope of Analysis

At each stage of the analysis, the scope needs to be clearly defined and cascaded down until the root causes of performance are established. This allows the identification of drivers, rather than focus on symptoms. *Fig. 6.2* shows the various levels of analysis. Each of these should be considered where appropriate. The key to quality analysis is thinking. Rather than trying to establish a set pattern to the analysis as a series of definitive steps, the art of asking the right questions needs to be developed as a recognisable skill. We will

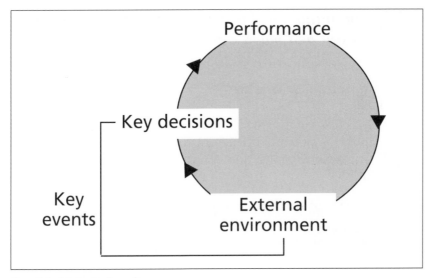

Fig. 6.1: Historical performance

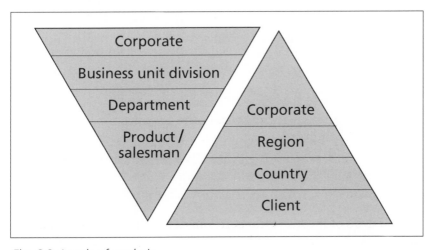

Fig. 6.2: Levels of analysis

establish the different forms of analysis and the various scopes that can be explored.

The starting point for the analysis should be the corporate whole, with further questions asked at the appropriate levels, such as business unit, divisional and market/region levels. Trends need to be analysed down to the most common denominator, which may be drilled down to individual product or service, and client level. The nature of the analysis will be dependent on how the company is structured in terms of reporting and management. If the analysis does not reflect the structure then there will be little value in the analysis as no accountability will be established.

Key Financial Parameters

The analysis of financial data should be from a strategic perspective. The various components of each of the elements of the variables will allow a "drilling" down to the root cause of the issues facing the organisation.

One of the key aims of private companies is to generate as much profit as possible from the assets under their control. This can be measured using the Return on Capital Employed (ROCE) ratio.

ROCE (%) = (operating profit/capital employed) x 100

where the
- Operating profit can be defined as the profit before interest and tax, and
- Capital employed is fixed assets plus net current assets (stock + debtors + cash – short term liabilities)

The ROCE provides an indication of the level of profit that has been squeezed out of the assets. One would argue that if ROCE falls below the interest rates, then the organisation would be better off putting its funds into a bank account. There are many counter arguments to this, which we shall not delve into here.

Profit and Loss Statement

Fig. 6.3 shows the various components of the analysis of the profit and loss accounts.

The profit and loss figure can vary due to either:

- revenue (1), or
- costs (2).

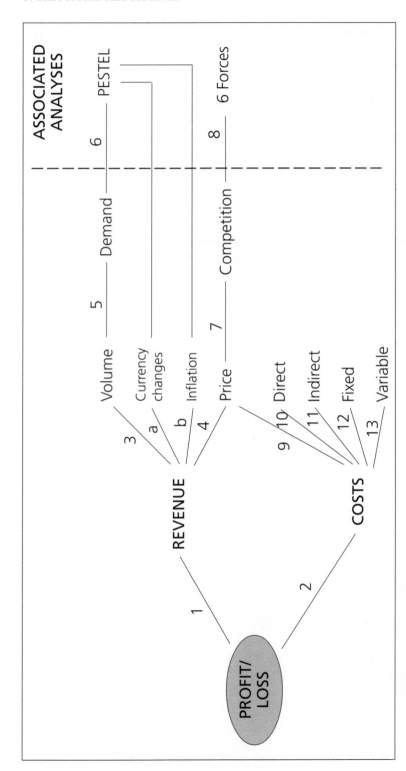

Fig. 6.3: Profit and loss account analysis

Revenue can be influenced by:

- currency changes (a), or
- inflation (b).

A key ratio that helps enhance understanding of the reasons behind the change in revenue performance of an organisation is:

Sales growth – This tends to set the scene for the rest of the analysis. This can be directly linked to the external analysis to identify the links between market trends and organisation trends. The sales growth will also allow a determination in the market shares of the key players. Notes to the accounts, in the financial report, will provide relevant data to enable this analysis to be carried out by:

- product type
- geographical scope.

The sales growth is calculated as follows:

Sales growth (%) = $((\text{sales}(n) - \text{sales}(n-1))/\text{sales}(n-1)) \times 100$
where n represents the current time period.

The primary causes of revenue movement is:

- volume (3), and
- price (4).

The volume of a product or service ensures that real quantity changes are monitored and accounted for. The volume changes as a result of demand (5), which in turn is influenced by the external environment, the PESTEL factors (6). This enables the analyst to directly link organisational performance to changes in the external environment.

Revenue changes might be due to price fluctuations which are caused by changes in costs (9) and due to changes in the competitive environment (7), such as predatory pricing by new entrants or existing competitors. This should be linked to the 6 force analysis (8), including the competitor appraisal. Price may also reflect changes in inflation.

Organisations need to link the revenue to the direct cost base of manufacture or delivery of service to determine the gross margin.

The gross margin indicates the difference between the selling price of goods or services and the cost of manufacture or production. It gives an indication of the potential profitability of an organisation. Trends in gross margin demonstrate what might be happening in either sales or costs.

Gross margin is calculated as follows:

Gross margin (%) = gross profit x 100/sales

Operating margin is a measure of how much profit is made from a business, net of expenses, thus giving an indication as to how much is available for distribution to shareholders, Inland Revenue, etc. The trends in operating margin are a function of trends in gross margin and expenses. The operating margin is:

Operating margin (%) = operating profit/sales

The cost structure (9) of the company has a major impact on pricing. However, it is not guaranteed that this will be reflected in the price.

Cost is categorised in a couple of different ways:

• fixed (12) and variable costs (13)
• direct (10) and indirect costs (11)

Each of these elements may need to be broken down into the smallest components as shown in *Fig. 6.2*.

Expenses to sales – Expenses generally comprise administration, marketing and distribution costs. Expenses to sales ratio provides a measure of how efficient the organisation is in delivering its product to the customer. Trends in the expenses to sales ratio should be interpreted in relation to sales growth trends. As sales growth changes, this needs to be reflected in the expenses. Notes to the accounts sometimes provide details on the constituent components of expenses, and these may well be worth exploring.

Expense-sales ratio (%) = (gross profit – operating profit)/sales

In addition to the above, analysis of the profit and loss account should also include employee ratios, such as:

Sales per employee – Provides a broad indication of productivity, and needs to be combined with,

Sales per employee = sales/number of employees

Operating profit per employee = operating profit/number of employees

Balance Sheet

Fig. 6.4 shows the various components of the balance sheet.

Management has greatest day-to-day control over current assets, and the following ratios help in the assessment of these:

Stock days – This provides an approximate measure of the number of days' sales in stock. There are no real optimum levels that we should be looking for, but certainly the trends need to be monitored and analysed. Though working capital needs to be minimised, this should not be at the expense of customer needs. Differences exist in the optimum levels depending on the nature of the industry:

Stock days = (stock/cost of sales) x 365

Debtor days – This provides an indication of the number of days' sales for which payment is outstanding. Management needs to minimise the number of days to ensure a positive cashflow is maintained. Different industries have different levels of acceptable debt. The analysis should explore what happens if suddenly the level of debtors increases, particularly if the company begins to export:

Debtor days = (debtors/sales) x 365

Creditor days – This provides an indication of the number of days' purchases for which payment is still due:

Creditor days = (trade creditors/cost of sales) x 365

Fixed Asset Ratios

Analysis of the fixed assets is more difficult to interpret due to the lack of control at operational management level, and is much more

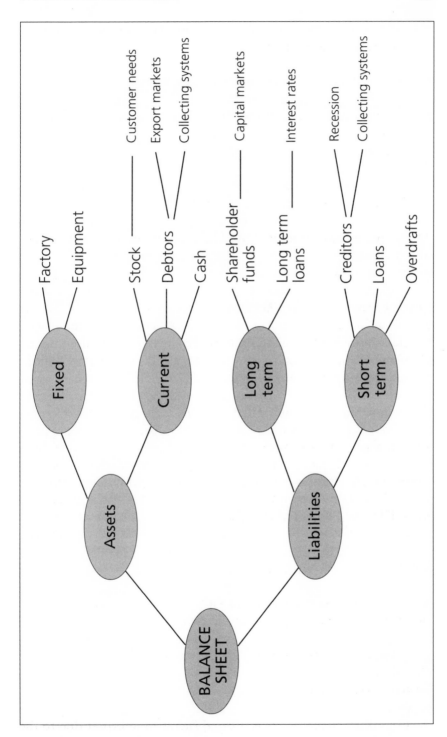

Fig. 6.4: Balance sheet analysis

part of the longer term strategic decision making process. The key ratios to look at are:

Fixed assets/sales – If this ratio increases it may be due either to heavier investment or a fall in sales, indicating that short term measures are not be taken, such as reducing capacity. The analysis needs to tie in very closely with trends in sales. Longer timeframes are ideal for this analysis:

Fixed assets/sales = (fixed assets/sales) x 100

Asset turn – This ratio provides an indication of the value of sales generated by the capital employed in the business:

Asset turn = sales/capital employed

Long Term Liquidity Ratios

Capital gearing ratio gives an indication of the ability of the company to finance its operations in the longer term. The general rule is that the gearing ratio should not exceed 100%, thus allowing payment of creditors. If the ratio is very high the ability to finance further expansion may be constrained. The ratio is linked to strategic decisions and provides a clue as to where major investments have taken place:

Capital gearing ratio = (total debt/shareholders' funds) x 100

Short Term Liquidity Ratios

Acid ratio gives an indication of the ability of the organisation to pay or finance its short term or immediate liabilities:

Acid ratio = (debtors + cash)/liabilities

Current ratio includes stock as a current asset into the acid ratio:

Current ratio = current assets/current liabilities

Analysis of these ratios give an indication of the management's ability to respond to potential problems at an early stage, and ensuring adequate action is taken. Poor liquidity ratios usually suggest poor management skills.

Key Events Analysis

As shown in *Fig. 6.1*, in addition to the performance of the organisation, the key events in the history of the organisation should also be plotted and their impact explored. The key events analysis has two perspectives:

Internal

The key decisions taken by the company during the time period under analysis. In fact, the key decisions might need to go beyond the analytical timeframe to allow for any time lags to be taken into account.

Typical decisions that need to be considered can be thought of in terms of the McKinseys 7 Ss *(Fig. 6.5)*.

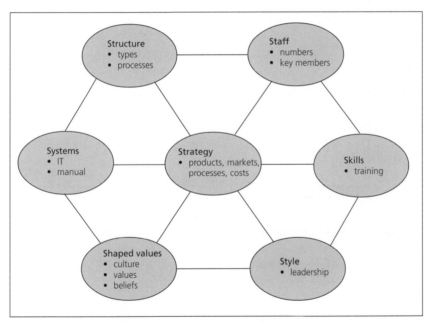

Fig. 6.5: McKinsey's 7 Ss

Structure – Changes in organisation structure, reporting mechanisms
Strategy – Changes in products, markets, processes
Systems – Changes to information technology or manual systems
Staff/Skills – Changes in key staff, skills mix
Leadership – Change in leadership and style of leadership
Culture – Changes in attitudes, values and beliefs

External

Key drivers and changes in the environment should be noted from the PESTEL analysis and 6 forces analysis. This can encompass dates at which new entrants came to a market, existing players left, etc.

The key events can be gathered from discussion with people who have been in the organisation, as well as secondary data, such as Economist reports. These should then be plotted on the graph showing the historical performance *(Fig. 6.6)*.

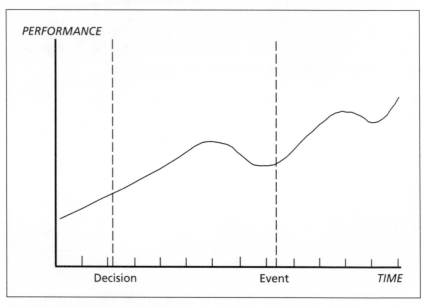

Fig. 6.6: Performance analysis

Summary of Key Ratios

OVERALL
a. ROCE (%) = (operating profit/capital employed) x 100

PROFIT & LOSS STATEMENT
b. Sales growth (%) = ((sales(n) – sales(n-1))/sales(n-1)) x 100
c. Gross margin (%) = gross profit x 100/sales
d. Operating margin (%) = operating profit/sales
e. Expense-sales ratio (%) = (gross profit – operating profit)/sales
f. Sales per employee = sales/number of employees
g. Operating profit per employee = operating profit/number of employees

BALANCE SHEET

i. Stock days = (stock/cost of sales) x 365

j. Debtor days = (debtors/sales) x 365

k. Creditor days = (trade creditors/cost of sales) x 365

l. Fixed assets/sales = (fixed assets/sales) x 100

m. Asset turn = sales/capital employed

n. Capital gearing ratio = (total debt/shareholders' funds) x 100

o. Acid ratio = (debtors + cash)/liabilities

p. Current ratio = current assets/current liabilities

Activity 7

The following is a set of financial data and key strategic decisions taken by ABC Limited. Using the Historical Analysis format, identify the key issues being highlighted by the analysis.

INCOME (UK£m)	1989	1990	1991	1992	1993	1994	1995	1996	1997	1998
Sales	52	84	116	147	168	195	220	257	271	293
Cost of Goods	24	35	47	63	70	80	79	96	100	104
Depreciation	1	2	4	5	7	10	11	12	12	12
GROSS INCOME	26	48	65	79	91	106	130	149	159	177
Total Operating Exp.	41	68	94	120	144	165	185	222	232	255
OPERATING INCOME	11	17	22	28	25	31	35	34	39	38
Number of employees	611	1265	1844	1926	2124	2456	3111	3670	3899	4756

Key Strategic Decisions (KSD)

	Year	Key Event/Strategic Decision
KSD1	1990	First US store opened.
KSD2	1994	Group opens 6 new shops in the UK through the year and introduces new organisation structure.
KSD3	1995	New marketing strategy, focused on product development and Internet. Opens 77 stores in US through the year.
KSD4	1996	New management team. Slowdown announced in US and closure of 10 stores. Focus on higher spending customers.
KSD5	1997	New rationalisation strategy announced, focusing on products and outlets.
KSD6	1998	New CEO takes over from founder. Restructuring announced – refitting 400 outlets, cutting stocks and streamlining the distribution system.

Data Presentation

The quality of analysis depends on the presentation of data, and its ability to communicate and manage large amounts of data into something of value. A good reference for presenting data is *Presenting Statistics* by Lawrence Witzling and Robert Greenstreet. This text is recommended for the analyst prior to carrying out any data analysis.

Solution to Activity 7

RATIOS	1989	1990	1991	1992	1993	1994	1995	1996	1997	1998
Sales growth		64%	37%	28%	14%	16%	12%	17%	6%	8%
Gross Profit margin	51%	56%	56%	54%	54%	54%	59%	58%	59%	60%
Operating profit margin	21%	20%	19%	19%	15%	16%	16%	13%	14%	13%
Sales /employee (000s)	84	67	63	77	79	80	71	70	69	62

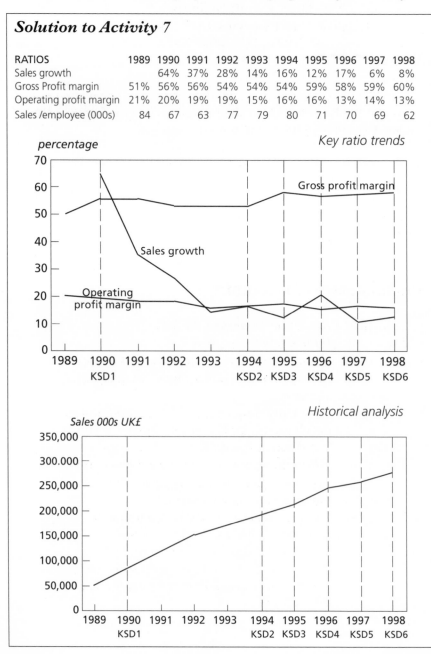

Analysis Points

Sales Revenue Graph

1. Not sufficient information available for 1989 to 1994 to reach any meaningful conclusions.
2. Benefits of KSD2 appear in 1997.
3. KSD3 involves major expansion. No major growth in overall sales performance is experienced by the organisation. It appears as if growth slows down in 1996.

Ratio Analysis Graph

1. After opening first US store in 1990, there appears to be little evidence of sales growth, though more data is needed to come to any meaningful conclusion.
2. In 1994, ABC opens new shops in UK, with increase in growth one year later.
3. In 1995, the organisation opens 77 new stores, but a year later growth drops. Why?
4. In 1997, the gross profit margin improves one year after a rationalisation strategy is announced.
5. Sales begin to grow in 1997, perhaps as a result of focusing on higher spending customers.

Analytical Steps

1 Collect main items of data, such as company reports, marketing data, operational data and other performance related data
2 Identify trends in the data
3 Calculate the key ratios
4 Identify the key events from the internal and external perspective
5 State the strengths and weaknesses of the ability of the organisation and its management to achieve strategic objectives and goals, and meet the challenges of a changing environment

Summary

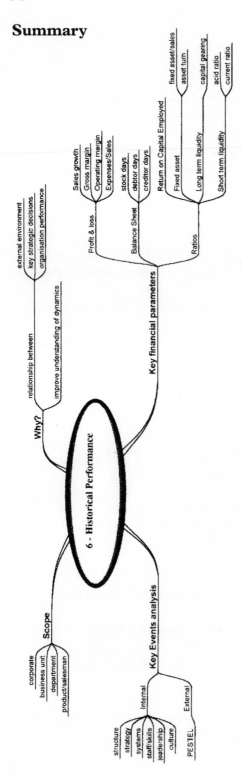

7

DETERMINING LEADERSHIP STYLE

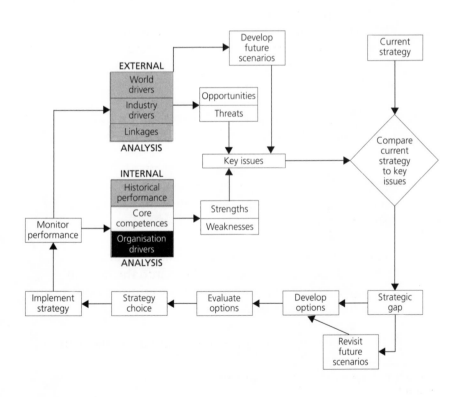

INPUTS
- leader attributes
- follower needs
- situation assessment

Tannenbaum & Schmidt model

OUTPUTS
- strengths, weaknesses

*"When an organisation finds itself in conflict with
another organisation, it is the strategic skill of the leader
that will determine the outcome of events."*
Sun Tzu

CONCEPTS

Defining Leadership

Leadership is defined as "the process of moving a group of people in
the same direction, largely through non-coercive means". The role
of leadership is to:

- Build and lead a team of individuals to achieve collective
  effort to solve problems.
  The goal is to be recognised as a valued member of the
  team, not necessarily the team leader. Being able to make
  things happen. The ability to set priorities and manage the
  time resource.

- Establish appropriate goals and objectives.
  Take in all information, sort by relevance and consider
  rationally.

- Understand the environment and resources.
  Consider the variables that are likely to impact on the
  decisions.

- Create, articulate and passionately own a vision.
  Getting ideas out of the leader's head into the head of
  others. Being uncompromising, empowering and possessing
  values that will drive to be the best.

- Effectively decentralise, delegate and motivate the team.

Leadership and the Manager

When exploring and analysing leadership, the strategist should look
at whether the organisation possesses leaders or managers or both.
The key differences between a leader manager and a typical manager
are that leaders:

- Think in the longer term
- Create relevant links with elements of the external environment
- Influence beyond their immediate boundaries through their social and political skills
- Emphasise the importance, through application, of vision, values and motivation
- Challenge the current processes and situation, adapting where necessary

Leadership Variables

Research by Tannenbaum and Schmidt (ref. 7.1) *(see Fig 7.1)* has shown that there is no one style of leadership that is effective in all situations, and that the style to be adopted is dependent on the:

- leader
- follower, and
- situation.

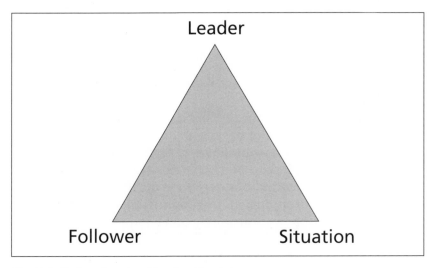

Fig. 7.1: Determinants of leadership style

(i) The leader

The leader will possess certain attributes that will enable the greatest impact to be made in a team situation and that will be unique to that particular leader. The key attributes *(Fig. 7.2)* are:

Ref. 7.1: Tannenbaum, R. and Schmidt, W., "How to Choose a Leadership Pattern", (Harvard Business Review, March/April, 1957)

Fig. 7.2: Leadership attributes

- **Intelligence –** Comprising industry and organisation knowledge
- **Motivation –** To drive the team members to unknown limits
- **Credibility and competence –** Possessing a reputation and track record, though this can be overcome by having a stronger combination of some of the other attributes
- **Implementation and management skills –** Made up of planning, budgeting, organising and controlling emotional stability
- **Social skills –** Understanding people by developing relationships through listening
- **Personal values –** Affirming values and reinforcing these within the team
- **Talent spotting skills –** having the ability to identify and encourage talents
- **Adaptability and flexibility of approach –** All great leaders are not attached to a particular approach. They will change approach as and when needed without hesitation

- **Warrior attitude** – Made up of sensitivity, confidence, commitment, timing, strength, self control and intuition *(Fig. 7.3)*.

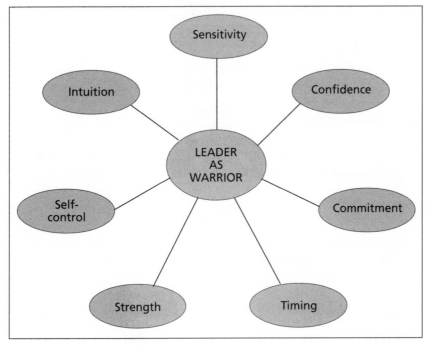

Figure 7.3: Warrior leaders

Another aspect to consider is the leader's ability to change or leadership style flexibility. Some styles of leadership may be so ingrained in an individual that there is little chance of change. Also some may have become so successful in different environments that they feel there is little need for change. Changes can be made in any of three elements, i.e. leadership qualities, followers' make-up or situational change.

Kotter (ref. 7.2) states that in today's complex and dynamic environments effective leadership is about:

a. Creating an agenda for change
- include a vision of what can and what should be
- include a vision that takes into account the legitimate long term interests of all parties involved

Ref. 7.2, Kotter, J. P., "The Leadership Factor", (Free Press, 1988)

• include a strategy for achieving the vision and taking into account the internal and external forces.

b. Building a strong implementation network
• building supportive relationships with key sources of power
• relationships to elicit co-operation, compliance and teamwork
• highly motivated core group of people
• core group committed to make a vision happen.

(ii) The Follower

The type of style is also dependent on the qualities of the people the leaders are trying to lead. Followers have needs based on:

• Need for independence
• Ability to assume responsibility
• Tolerance for ambiguity
• Understanding of goals and objectives
• Ability to function as part of a team.

These elements are further explored in Chapter 9 (staff and skills).

(iii) The Situation

The situation itself will determine the ideal way to lead. The variables that need to be taken into consideration are:

a   The type of organisation – in terms of size, geographical spread
b   The effectiveness of team members – in terms of experience and capability
c   The nature of the problem – this is also dependent on the stage of the lifecycle the company is in (*Fig. 7.4*). At different stages of the lifecycle the type of leader needed is quite different.
During the start-up phase, the leader needs to be a visionary, possessing great communication skills and also having "scrooge" like tendencies to ensure that life is sustained for the organisation, without over committing in terms of financial resources. The attitude of the leader is focused on possessing a "killer instinct" in business terms,

	Birth	Growth	Maturity	Decline
Stage	Visionary	Visionary	Realist	Turnaround artist
Elements	• communicative • influential • "scrooge"	• information manager	• analytical • creative • change agent	• "streetfighter" • communicator • results focus
Profile	• "eye of the tiger"	"visible" "surfer on the crest"	"professional manager"	"fighter"

Fig. 7.4: Relevance of leadership types to lifecycle

making sacrifices to ensure the goals are met. As the organisation moves into growth, the leader needs to become more distant from the "doing" type of activities. At this stage they become more managers of information, being more visible to a growing organisation During maturity, creative skills become more of a necessity, as do the skills of making change happen. As a realist, the leader possesses a balanced view of the business with little or no emotional attachment to one particular type of strategy. Once the business goes into decline, the "streetfighter" comes into his or her own. The leader will ensure that there is no way the organisation will die without a fight.

d The time available to make a decision.

Different Types of Leadership Style

There are many ways of categorising leadership styles, usually based on some of the key tasks of the leader. We shall look at styles based on one of the key tasks of a leader, i.e. decision making. Tannenbaum and Schmidt's model is based on the different emphasis on decision making. *Fig. 7.5* shows an adapted version of Tannenbaum and Schmidt's model. The style depends on the level of involvement of team members and the degree of input from the leader. Decision making focused on the left side of the model (Type I) represents a more autocratic style of leadership, whereas greater focus on the righthand side is more democratic (Type V).

Within an organisation a layer of leaders can be created with an emphasis on diffusion of power, thus empowering managers at all levels of the organisation, ensuring that there is flexibility and an environment that encourages creativity and challenges the status quo. In association with this, the organisation also should be able to consider the methods of producing and developing leaders both internally and externally. These include:

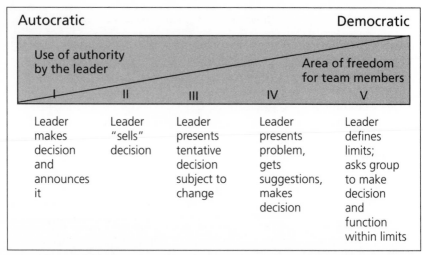

Figure 7.5: Tannenbaum & Schmidt's model of leadership style. Adapted from Modern Management, *Samuel C. Certo, (Allyn and Bacon, 1994)*

- Developing effective recruiting processes
- Creating an effective work environment
- Offering challenging opportunities within the organisation
- Ability to identify and develop potential leaders at an early stage
- Process for planned development

Criteria for Success

One of the problems with a mobile workforce is that leaders too become highly mobile. This then raises the question of how to assess the success of particular leaders, as they may well have left the role by the time any form of valued judgement can be made. The criteria for success revolves around the effectiveness of the leader. However, leaders such as Adolph Hitler were highly effective but, to the majority, would not have been deemed to be successful. In addition to being effective, leaders also should be morally correct in the business context. This raises the point that this is success from one perspective, one that the leader may not be concerned about. In the corporate world the moral standpoint is vital, as the people (staff) do not have to be there.

To achieve success in the corporate world, the leader needs to ensure that the following are built into their leadership style:

- A capacity for helping the team fulfil to a maximum the potential of team members, by encouraging and developing the creative dimension within individuals.
- A respect for the law, local and national customs and traditions, thus endearing the leader to the masses.
- The building of networks and relationships to achieve the objectives of the organisation.

Obstacles to Success

Many obstacles exist to stop the leader being successful.

First, the nature of the crises may well stop the leader being able to make any significant impact. In March 1998, President Yeltsin of Russia appointed Kiriyenko as Prime Minister to replace Victor Chernomyrdin. After five months Kiriyenko was replaced by Chernomyrdin himself. The nature of the crises facing Russia was such that immediate results were sought. If a leader is expected to change a whole nation within five months, what are the prospects for a new manager trying to make turnaround happen in a company?

Second, the size and complexity of the organisation may prohibit the leader from being able to influence sufficient layers of management to make change worthwhile. However, this would test the political skills of the leader. In addition, the systems and processes in the organisation may be a hindrance that will stop the leader from addressing the issues, thus the leader may need to make organisational changes, and maybe share leadership tasks, before any significant impact can be made.

Third, specialisation creates artificial boundaries that may hinder leaders, but encourage managers to prosper. This factor may also stop potential leaders from growing appropriate networks and relationships, both internally and externally of the organisation.

Leadership Development

In assessing the effectiveness of leaders, and their strengths and weaknesses, the strategist must also consider the process of leadership development. Morrison (ref. 7.3) talks of the balancing of three components for sustained leadership development. These are *(Fig. 7.6)*:

Ref. 7.3: Morrison, A. M., "The New Leaders", (Jossey-Bass Publishers, 1992)

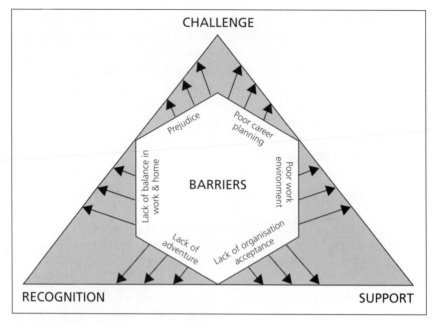

Fig. 7.6: Components of leadership development

1. Challenge
An organisation needs to ensure that the potential leaders are tested regularly through challenging assignments that ensure the individual grows and is exposed to the difficulties and stresses to be faced in a leadership role.

2. Recognition
This includes acknowledgement and rewards for being successful.

3. Support
Sufficient resources, both financial and people, should be made available to the potential leader so that an opportunity to succeed presents itself, as opposed to providing a challenging assignment that is doomed to fail due to lack of support.

Morrison goes on to state that the barriers to leadership development are:

- **Prejudice** – Assumptions people hold which prevent them from seeing the new, which is clearly the requirement of a leader.

- **Poor career planning** – Leaders do not just happen, and the only person responsible for becoming a leader is the individual.
- **Poor work environment** – The work environment should encourage creative and innovative thinking that also allows the potential leader to fail, so as to learn.
- **Lack of organisation acceptance** – Leadership is a political game, and the key is to win the key influencers.
- **Lack of adventure** – Potential leaders may well be afraid to step outside their world of comfort, thus preventing the development of the networks and links required.
- **Lack of balance between work and home** – Part of the role of the organisation is to provide an environment that is balanced and does not encourage development at the expense of family life.

Analytical Steps

1 Identify the leaders and managers in your organisation.
2 Assess on a table whether each individual demonstrates the traits of a leader or of a manager, justifying your reasons.
3 Analyse the attributes of each of the leaders, assessing their relevance to the situation.
4 Using the previous analyses of the external environment, assess the relevance of the style adopted.
5 Identify the needs of the teams and explore how they differ from team to team.
6 Assess the fit between the follower and leader
7 Determine the Leadership Profile, Follower Independence and Situation Appraisal using *Fig. 7.7.*
8 Plot the assessment of the current situation and Follower Independence using *Fig. 7.8.*
9 Take the assessment from (8) and determine the desired level of Leadership Attribute.
10 Compare the desired Leadership attributes (9) with the actual, as assessed in (7).
11 Identify the strengths and weaknesses of the different styles.
12 Determine the level of commitment from the organisation for the development of leaders and state as a strength or weakness *(Fig 7.9)*.
13 State all strengths and weaknesses of the leadership.

LEADERSHIP ANALYSIS

	Low	Medium	High
Leadership profile			
• Intelligence			
• Motivation			
• Credibility			
• Implementation & management skills			
• Social skills			
• Personal values			
• Talent spotting skills			
• Adaptability & flexibility of approach			
• Warrior attitude			
Overall leadership attributes	Low	Medium	High

	Low	Medium	High
Follower independence			
• Need for independence			
• Ability to assume responsibility			
• Tolerance for ambiguity			
• Understand goals & objectives			
• Ability to function as part of a team			
Overall follower independence	Low	Medium	High

SITUATION APPRAISAL

Type of organisation				
• Size	Small	Medium	Large	
• Geographical spread	Narrow	Medium	Broad	
Effectiveness of team members				
• Experience	Low	Medium	High	
• Capability	Low	Medium	High	
Stage of lifecycle of company	Birth	Growth	Maturity	Decline
Time availability	Short	Medium	Long	
Overall situation appraisal	Poor	Medium	Good	

7.7: Questionnaire for assessing leadership

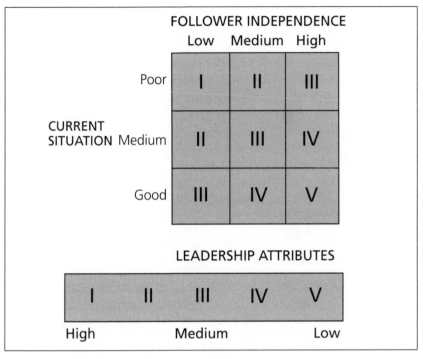

7.8: *Assessing leadership style*

Challenging environment
1 Number of projects designed
2 Internal processes for progressing
  level of difficulty in projects
3 Degree of management
  commitment to designing
  projects for potential leaders
4 Level of monitoring of progress
  of potential leaders

ASSESSMENT OF CHALLENGING ENVIRONMENT   LOW   MEDIUM   HIGH

Recognition
1 Process for acknowledging
  success of potential leaders
2 Reward systems for success

ASSESSMENT OF LEVEL OF RECOGNITION   LOW   MEDIUM   HIGH

Support
1 Level of financial support
  provided for projects for potential
  leaders
2 Level of people support provided
  for projects for potential leaders

ASSESSMENT OF LEVEL OF SUPPORT   LOW   MEDIUM   HIGH

7.9: *Leadership development assessment*

Summary

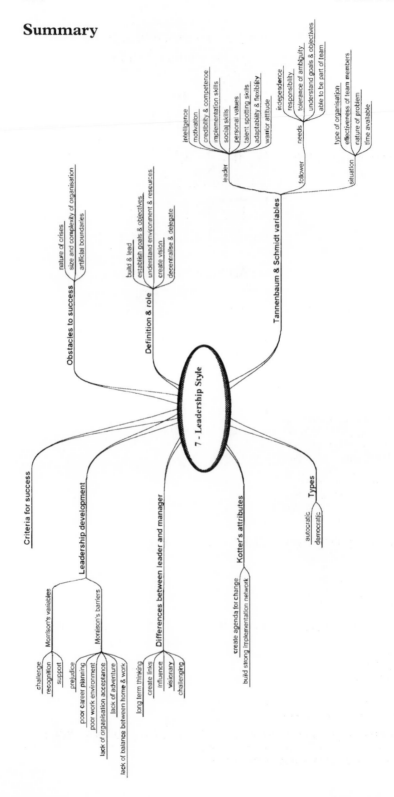

7 - Leadership Style

Obstacles to success
- nature of crises
- size and complexity of organisation
- artificial boundaries

Definition & role
- build & lead
- establish goals & objectives
- understand environment & resources
- create vision
- decentralise & delegate

Tannenbaum & Schmidt variables
- leader
  - intelligence
  - motivation
  - credibility & competence
  - implementation skills
  - social skills
  - personal values
  - talent spotting skills
  - adaptability & flexibility
  - warrior attitude
- follower
  - independence
  - responsibility
  - tolerance of ambiguity
  - understand goals & objectives
  - able to be part of team
- situation
  - type of organisation
  - effectiveness of team members
  - nature of problem
  - time available

Criteria for success

Leadership development
- Morrison's variables
  - challenge
  - recognition
  - support
  - prejudice
  - poor career planning
  - poor work environment
- Morrison's barriers
  - lack of organisation acceptance
  - lack of adventure
  - lack of balance between home & work

Differences between leader and manager
- long term thinking
- create links
- influence
- visionary
- challenging

Kotter's attributes
- create agenda for change
- build strong implementation network

Types
- autocratic
- democratic

8

CULTURE, VALUES AND BELIEFS

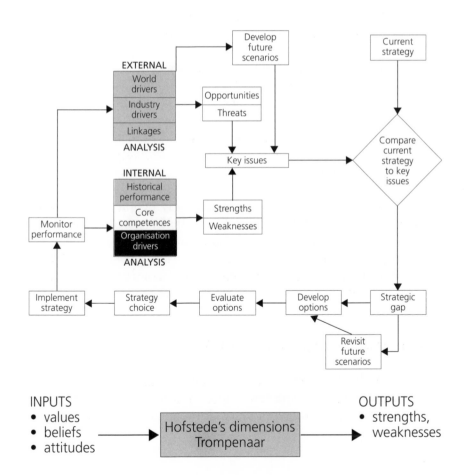

"Preserve the best, and improve the rest."
Al Neuharth

CONCEPTS

One of the most neglected areas in strategic analysis comprises the softer areas of strategy. These in essence represent the "glue" that sticks the various components of the organisation together, in the form of the culture, values and beliefs that are held by the people in the organisation.

Defining Corporate Culture

Corporate culture can be defined in the following ways:

> *"The deeper level of basic assumptions and beliefs that are shared by members of an organisation, that operate unconsciously and define a basic 'taken for granted' [that] fashions an organisation's view of itself and its environment." – Edgar Schein, "Organisation Culture and Leadership"*

> *"The way we do things around here." – Deal and Kennedy, "Corporate Cultures: The risks and rituals of corporate life."*

Essentially, the corporate culture is the way people behave in an organisation through the assumptions and beliefs that the individuals hold at both a personal and organisational level. The challenge for the manager is to address issues related to the fact that cultural change tends to lag behind strategic change and that, more often than not, culture controls the manager rather than the manager controlling the culture.

National and Corporate Culture

Culture can be described in terms of national differences as well as corporate differences. The national dimension has become more relevant as organisations adopt more global and internationally based strategies.

> *"When people set up an organisation they will*
> *typically borrow from models or ideals that are*
> *familiar to them. The organisation ... is a subjective*
> *construct and its employees will give meaning to their*
> *environment based on their particular cultural*
> *programming."* – Fons Trompenaar

While organisational culture is clearly shaped by technologies and markets, it is also influenced greatly by the cultural preferences of both its leaders and employees.

Trompenaar, in his research (ref. 8.1), considered three aspects of organisational structure that are particularly important in creating corporate culture. These are:

1. The general relationships between employees and the organisation
2. The systems of authority that define superiors and subordinates
3. The shared views of the organisation's purpose, destiny, goals, etc.

Trompenaar also identified four types of corporate culture, which show considerable variations in the way(s) people think, motivate, resolve conflict and reward people. Again, the creation of these types brings with it the risk of stereotyping, so the international manager must strive for a deeper understanding of local culture and should never forget the danger of oversimplifying a situation.

Types of Corporate Culture

The four types of corporate culture are described using the following metaphors :

1. The Family
2. The Eiffel Tower
3. The Guided Missile
4. The Incubator

Ref 8.1: Trompenaar, Fons "Riding the Waves of Culture", (Nicholas Brealey Publishing, 1993)

1 The Family Culture

Trompenaar uses this metaphor to describe a culture that is both personal, encouraging close relationships, and hierarchical; the "father" of the organisation has greater experience and authority than those around him. The resulting corporate culture is power-oriented and (ideally) intimate and benign. This type of culture is favoured by the Japanese, who tend to recreate aspects of the traditional Japanese family within the organisation. For the Japanese, one of the most important business virtues is *amae*, a form of love between people of different ranks, where the senior shows indulgence to the junior who in turn shows respect. The ideal relationship is *sempai-kohai*, akin to that between an older and younger brother.

Relationships within the power-oriented family culture are usually diffuse. The "father" or senior is influential in all situations, whether inside or outside the workplace. In this type of culture, people are more concerned with intuitive rather than rational knowledge, and the development – rather than the deployment – of individuals is stressed. Criticisms are seldom made publicly, 'family business' is kept behind closed doors and care is always taken to avoid public loss of face. Due to the importance people place on their relationships, they may well be motivated more by praise than by money.

The family culture finds a home readily in countries such as India, Spain and France.

2 The Eiffel Tower Culture

This metaphor is used to describe a corporate culture that has a formal bureaucracy, with various roles and functions determined in advance. This culture is narrow at the top, broad and stable at the base, and is rigid and strong. In this culture, structure is more important than function.

A key difference between this and the family culture is that, within the Eiffel Tower, the leader is only incidentally a person; more accurately, he or she is a role. Relationships, therefore, tend to be specific and status is ascribed. The Eiffel Tower is a depersonalised, rational system in which careers are greatly assisted by the acquisition of appropriate qualifications. At each level of the hierarchy, every role is clearly identified, rated for its difficulty and complexity, and awarded a salary that reflects its status. In essence, the Eiffel Tower culture rejects everything the family culture readily accepts.

The Eiffel Tower corporate culture is popular in Germany, Austria and Denmark.

3 The Guided Missile Culture

This is at once egalitarian, impersonal and task-oriented. These tasks are usually undertaken by cross-disciplinary teams or project groups. Unlike the Eiffel Tower culture, tasks are not predetermined; team members are expected to do whatever is necessary to ensure success, even if it is unclear at first how that might be achieved.

Groups assembled within the guided missile culture will have leaders or co-ordinators, although they will often know less about specific subjects than the specialists they have brought together; they need, therefore, to treat these experts with obvious respect. Such groups are usually temporary, breaking up once the task is complete, and so relationships are generally fleeting. Consequently, this culture lacks the affectionate, intimate nature of the family culture and, in this sense, could be regarded as neutral.

Members of the guided missile culture need to know how to "get on" with others quickly, to establish themselves as an integral part of a team, and be problem rather than discipline centred. Motivation tends to be intrinsic, in that people are driven by an enthusiasm to solve the problem. In the final analysis, in the guided missile culture individual value is determined by performance – the ability to contribute significantly to the jointly desired outcome.

This culture is valued by many organisations in Britain and the USA.

4 The Incubator Culture

This culture is built around the notion that the organisation is secondary to the fulfilment of the individual. The role of the organisation is to serve as an "incubator" for individual expression and self fulfilment. This type of culture acts as a sounding board for new ideas and tries to respond appropriately to new initiatives. It has minimal structure and hierarchy, and creates an environment of intense emotional commitment. However, this is a commitment to the importance of the work being undertaken rather than to the people involved. Everyone wants to contribute to the work at hand, and there is scant regard for personal security.

The incubator culture revels in the process of creation and innovation. As a result of the close relationships and shared enthusiasms, ideals and aspirations, people can be ruthlessly honest. The informal, spontaneous, dynamic nature of this cultural type usually limits its size – it is difficult to communicate in the required manner with hundreds of people – and often the life expectancy of the organisation.

Typical examples of incubator cultures are startup firms in Silicon Valley, although the country that scored highest in this regard in Trompenaar' research was Sweden.

Types of National Culture

> "Culture still seems like a luxury item to most
> managers, a dish on the side. In fact, culture
> pervades and radiates meanings into every aspect of
> the enterprise. Culture patterns the whole field of
> business relationships." – Fons Trompenaar

An increasing awareness of the notion – and reality – of the global market has led many businesses to expand into previously unknown territory, especially (although not limited to) the emerging markets of the Indian sub-continent, Southeast Asia and China. Few businesses appear to achieve excellence in these new environments. For example, reports state that of the 3,000 UK-based companies currently working in India, only 50% felt that they were being successful. Only 11% of American companies working there could report the same. This failure to achieve excellence is not due to a lack of technical expertise, but rather is rooted in an inability to understand and manage the key elements of the national culture involved. The notion that there is "one best way to manage" has been laid to rest by globalisation – at least within those organisations which are leading the way.

As the movement towards the globalisation of business continues, managers of multinational and international companies assume greater responsibility for managing individuals and groups with different cultural backgrounds, and with different societal values affecting their attitudes, behaviours and interpersonal relationships. It is important that managers understand these differences with respect to how they affect the work situation, and how they may call for different approaches to managing and different styles of leadership.

Management and leadership styles are inextricably linked to the ability to communicate effectively and create rapport; those working in foreign cultures have, therefore, to develop the ability to change their methods and manners of communication to suit the expectation(s) of the local culture. Quality of service can be measured not only by the outcome, but by the manner in which the outcome is achieved; the process is as important as the product and, in this context, suitability of process means matching it to the behaviours and requirements of the indigenous culture.

Understanding key elements of culture provides a valuable starting point for those seeking to develop the skills necessary to achieve excellence in international markets. The pioneering work of Geert Hofstede and Fons Trompenaar provides a solid foundation upon which these skills can be developed. We will focus on Hofstede's cultural dimensions:

Hofstede's Four Dimensions of National Culture

1 Power – Distance

This dimension is concerned with to what extent the culture encourages superiors to exert power.

In a High Power Distance culture inequality is accepted; the "Boss is the Boss". People know and accept their "place" and rarely disagree with their superiors. In such cultures, people **prefer** to work for managers who tell them what to do.

In a Low Power Distance culture, superiors and subordinates regard themselves as colleagues, and believe that inequalities should be minimised. People are rarely afraid to disagree and **expect** to be consulted before decisions are made.

2 Uncertainty – Avoidance

This dimension is concerned with how easily cultures cope with novelty.

In a Strong Uncertainty – Avoidance culture, people feel the need for clarity and order. They feel threatened by uncertainty and experience anxiety and stress in new and/or unpredictable situations. This tends to be combated by hard work, career stability and intolerance of deviancy. Company rules are rarely – if ever – broken, even if it would be in the company's best interests to do so.

In a Weak Uncertainty – Avoidance culture, the inherent uncertainty of life is more easily accepted. Rules are viewed pragmatically. Employees do not expect to work with a firm for long periods.

3 Individualism versus Collectivism

This dimension is concerned with the degree to which cultures encourage individual rather than group-centred concerns.

In an Individualist culture, the emphasis is on personal initiative and achievement; everyone has the right to a private life and opinion.

In a Collectivist culture, there is a much tighter social framework; the emphasis is on belonging and being a good group member. Collectivist involvement in the work organisation is a moral one and requires full commitment.

4 Masculinity versus Femininity

This dimension is concerned with the degree to which cultures highlight and value performance, money, material standards and ambition.

In a Masculine culture, the above are desired, striven for and applauded.

In a Feminine culture, it is a different quality of life that matters. People and the environment are important; service provides the motivation.

Shaping Behaviour

The behaviour of individuals within an organisation is a manifestation of the culture, which is shaped by the values, attitudes and beliefs of the individuals *(Fig. 8.1)*.

Analysis of the culture needs to explore the different facets of each of these to determine the strengths and weaknesses.

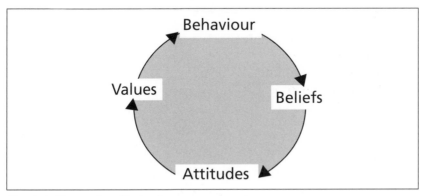

Fig. 8.1: The cycle of behaviour

Beliefs are driven by the individual's:

- religion
- philosophy
- faith

The beliefs held by the individual shape the attitudes towards other people. Attitudes are driven by:

- motivations
- aspirations
- expectations

A combination of an individual's beliefs and attitudes drive the values that then shape behaviour.

Defining Values

Values are the basis of the culture. These are the guiding principles that drive the organisation and represent the norms for standards of behaviour among team members and other stakeholders. Values also form the basis for decision making, but do not have to be thought of consciously.

A need exists to match the corporate values with the values of the individual to ensure commitment as opposed to compliance towards achieving the corporate goals.

Values have many components such as:

- People
- Customers and suppliers
- Quality
- Social responsibility
- Competitiveness
- Productivity
- Systems
- Innovation
- Profitability.

Cultures for the 21st Century

A dynamic environment with a high level of uncertainty attached requires a culture that encourages individuals to express themselves in a creative way. Rather than a culture, we may be talking more of a **corporate religion**. A **corporate religion** is an expression of a set of values and beliefs that people commit to almost in a spiritual manner, where leaders are seen as role models, as opposed to possessors of power. Leaders are seen as people to emulate, rather than to be fearful of. The environment provides the base rules from where an expression of creativity can be made. Team members are encouraged to try and make mistakes, providing there are lessons learned from these mistakes, and the leaders actually care about the outcomes. Ideally, the values and beliefs should reflect the values and beliefs that the individual holds personally, so that an individual does not feel as if there are two opposing forces vying for his attention, ie home and work. The two environments should be part of one.

In order to encourage creativity and innovation within this **corporate religion**, a commitment is needed to having fun and being relaxed, as numerous studies have demonstrated that people are at their most creative in these type of environments.

Corporate Mindsets

Many organisations speak of corporate culture in a negative context. It is expressed as a reason for failure, more often than not. However, corporate culture can be, and in fact is, a very powerful positive force that takes an organisation towards its goal like a missile homing in on a target, if managed and led effectively. Certain aspects of culture are responsible for the failure of strategy, but these are easier to rectify than the corporate culture. The negative elements of culture lie in the **Corporate Mindset**.

The **Corporate Mindset** is the set of assumptions and prejudices that a company holds, while leaders attempt to hold on for power. These assumptions are the result of history and experience, and past successes. Though it is important for an organisation to understand why it has been successful in the past, the danger is that as the environment progresses, the successful organisation rests on its laurels.

The distinction between the Corporate Mindset and Culture is made so that an organisation can retain the very positive elements of culture, but lose the prejudices and assumptions that prevent it from being creative and innovative.

Analytical Steps

1 Identify the characteristics of culture *(Fig. 8.2)* that are most prevalent in your organisation by interviewing:
   - employees
   - customers
   - suppliers
   - leaders
   - competitors
2 Ascertain whether these are Corporate or National dimensions, or both.
3 Identify the assumptions and prejudices within the organisation, as reflected in projects, that represent the corporate mindset.
4 Define the corporate values in terms of the various components, both as stated by the organisation and as perceived by the people *(Fig. 8.3)*.

ATTRIBUTES	FAMILY	EIFFEL	GUIDED MISSILE	INCUBATOR	NATIONAL CORPORAT
Leadership type	I	II / III	III / IV	V	
1. Type of personal relationships	Close	Distant	Distant	Close	National
2. Leadership type					
3. Level of respect for power:	High	High	Low	Low	
• Is inequality accepted?	Yes	Yes	No	No	
• Are people consulted?	No	No	Yes	Yes	
• To what extent are superiors and subordinates treated as colleagues?	Low	Medium	High	High	
4. Basis of knowledge	Intuitive	Specialist	Specialist	Specialist	
5. Reward mechanism	Self-esteem	Position	Financial	Financial	
6. Level of flexibility in responsibility	High	Low	Medium	High	
7. Importance of boundaries	Low	High	Medium	Low	
8. Importance of individuals	High	Low	Medium	High	National
• Are individuals allowed to show initiative?	Sometimes	Sometimes	Yes	Yes	
• Does everyone have a right to a 'personal life'?	No	Yes	No	Yes	
9. Internal competitiveness	Low	Medium	High	High	
10. Attitude to risk	Medium	Low	High	High	National
• Are people threatened by uncertainty and risk?	Sometimes	Yes	No	No	
• Do people expect to be with a firm for a long time?	Yes	Yes	No	No	
• Are people looking for clarity and order?	No	Yes	No	No	
11. Individual needs	Low	Low	Medium	High	National
• Is performance measured?	No	Yes	Yes	No	
• Are material needs vital?	No	Yes	Yes	Yes	
• Is quality of life vital?	Yes	No	No	Yes	
• Are people and environment important?	Yes	No	No	No	

Fig. 8.2: Cultural assessment

5 Agree the desired mindset and culture that is called for in today's competitive environment, using results from the external analysis.

6 Determine and list the strengths and weaknesses of the cultural dimensions against the desired position.

7 Prioritise the key strengths and weaknesses.

VALUE COMPONENT	STATED	PERCEIVED	GAP
1. People			
2. Customers			
3. Suppliers			
4. Quality			
5. Social responsibility			
6. Competitiveness			
7. Productivity			
8. Systems			
9. Innovation			
10. Profitability			

Fig. 8.3: Values gap analysis

Summary

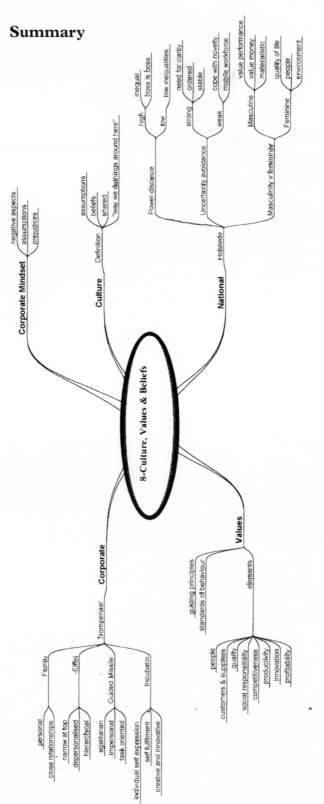

9

STAFF AND SKILLS

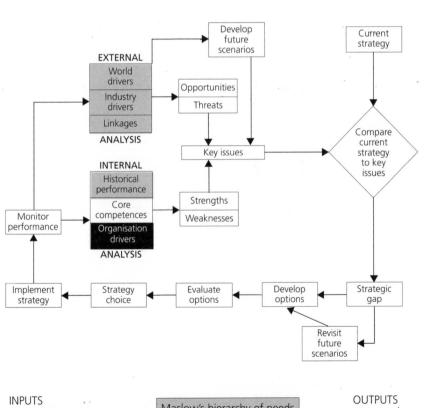

INPUTS
- individual traits
- group behaviour
- management systems
- skills

Maslow's hierarchy of needs
Organisational behaviour
Skills gap analysis

OUTPUTS
- strengths
- weaknesses

"The most single ingredient in the formula of success is knowing how to get along with people."
Theodore Roosevelt

CONCEPTS

No strategic analysis would be complete without a thorough appraisal of the most important resource of any organisation – its people and their skills. The capability of the organisation is directly related to the skills possessed by its people, and to those developed by the organisation.

In today's environment there is a need for greater empowerment of individuals so that decision making is faster and more appropriate for the situations being faced. This ties in with the systems and processes in the organisation, which is sometimes perceived as bureaucracy, and thus provides a slowing down in response to critical issues.

ANALYSING THE STAFF AS INDIVIDUALS

The key elements that need to be analysed *(Fig. 9.1)* are:

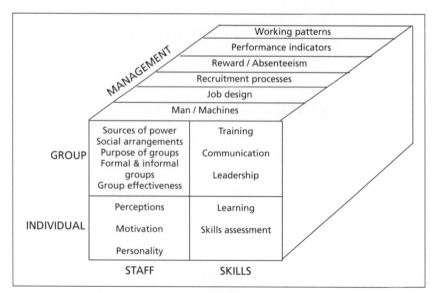

Fig. 9.1: Staff and skills appraisal cube

1. Perceptions *(Fig. 9.2)*

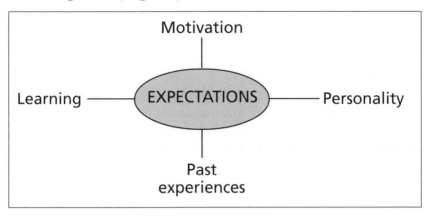

Fig. 9.2: Internal drivers of perception

Each individual sees different things in similar situations, leading to the raising or lowering of expectations, based on a number of internal factors. These are:

- Motivation and drives
- Personality
- Past experiences
- Learning and education

When the internal factors combine with the external environment they lead to a perception. The external stimuli which are most likely to affect perceptions are elements of the senses, such as:

- Sight
- Sound
- Taste
- Feel
- Smell

In terms of the analysis of staff, management need to understand the influences of perception on individuals in their teams and groups. The combination of different perceptions leads to a greater effectiveness of teams.

Possible sources of error in perceptions are:

- Focusing on inadequate and irrelevant information
- Seeing what you want to see
- Influenced by information too early in information gathering process
- Prejudices

These need to be determined in team members as possible strengths and weaknesses in the team make-up.

2. Motivations and Drives

A distinction should be made between motivation and drive. Motivation is the influence on human behaviour that is learned, which leads to the pursuit of particular goals because of social values. Drives, on the other hand, are determinants of human behaviour that are generally activated by deprivation. Both of these elements are combined into Maslow's (ref. 9.1) hierarchy of needs *(Fig. 9.3)*, which are indicators of drivers for team players that the leadership and management can identify as strengths and weaknesses. Maslow's hierarchy of needs are:

1 Physiological needs – such as sunlight, sex, food, water and other outcomes that are necessary to human survival.
2 Safety needs – protection from the threat of the environment.
3 Love needs – for relationships, affection, giving, and feeling of belonging.
4 Esteem needs – for strength, achievement, adequacy, confidence, independence, and for reputation, prestige, recognition, attention, importance, appreciation.
5 Self actualisation needs – for development of capability to the fullest potential.
6 Freedom of inquiry and expression needs – for free speech and encouraging justice.
7 The need to know and to understand – the need for curiosity, learning, experimenting and exploring.

Key elements that management needs to take into account when considering members needs are:

Ref 9.1: Maslow, Abraham, "Motivation and Personality", (Harper and Row, New York, 1970)

NEEDS	AREAS OF INFLUENCE
Physiological	Human existence
Safety	
Love	Relationships with others
Esteem	
Self actualisation	Ultimate human goal
Freedom of enquiry	Prerequisites for the satisfaction of other five needs
Need to know & understand	

Fig. 9.3: Maslow's hierarchy of needs

- A need is not an effective motivator unless the previous needs in the hierarchy are satisfied.
- A satisfied need is not a motivator.
- Dissatisfaction of these needs adversely affects mental health and affects the level of absenteeism.
- Humans have an innate desire to move up the hierarchy.
- The experience of self actualisation stimulates the desire for more.

Leadership and the strategist need to explore the degree of motivation in the organisation and the level of compatibility that exists between team members. Built into the strategy is the focus on motivation, enabling a balancing of the factors affecting human performance. Understanding the motivations leads to a better understanding of the decision making processes that individuals go through.

3. Personality

An individual's personality determines the style of leadership that needs to be adopted to maximise team and individual performance.

The German psychologist Carl Gustav Jung divided the human world into types of personality – EXTROVERTS and INTROVERTS.

Extroverts and Introverts *(Fig. 9.4)* each have seven personality traits, according to research carried out by Hans Jurgen Eysenck, another German psychologist.

There is a tendency for extroverts to need higher levels of stimulation, thus changing the demands on the leadership. Extroverts need and enjoy the presence of others, while introverts prefer the peace and quiet of solitude. These factors will clearly determine the style of management and the impact on performance of the organisation.

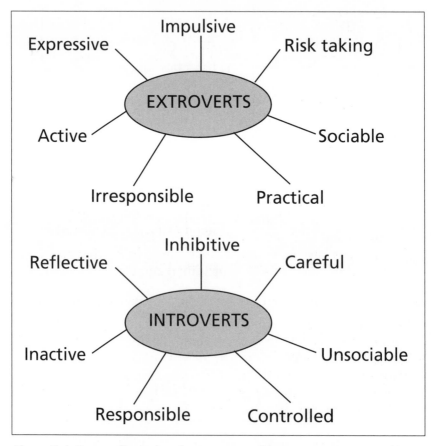

Figure 9.4: Personality traits of extroverts and introverts

ANALYSING THE STAFF AS A GROUP

1. Sources of Power

Power is defined as the potential influence that one person exerts over another. Many people hold a variety of sources of power. These may result from:

- Personal attractiveness
- Capacity to motivate
- Position
- Expertness
- Gift
- Reason
- Strength – Mao Tse Tung: *"Every communist must grasp the truth: political power grows out of the barrel of a gun"*
- Beliefs
- Coercion
- Intimidation
- Proximity to power
- Information
- Customs and tradition

A person holding a broader base of power is more likely to be effective in a management and leadership role. Identification of these individuals will enhance the likelihood of success of a strategy.

2. Social Structure and Arrangements

The social position of an individual is the relative position that a person holds and the value of the person as measured by a group of people. The positions are measured against the individual's ability to meet the expectations of the group.

The formal position of an individual is based on the post held by the person in an organisation, for which there exists a collection of rights and obligations. One of the primary sources of dissatisfaction in a team environment is the incongruence between the rewards and position held by an individual. In instances where the congruence is high, greater acceptance of responsibility and drive to succeed exists.

3. Purpose of Groups

Groups serve an organisational and individual need. The primary issue revolves around the level of potential conflict between the task objective of a group and the individual members' desire to satisfy their personal social objectives.

4. Formal and Informal Groups

Formal groups are groups in an organisation which have been consciously created to satisfy a collective goal or objective. Characteristics of formal groups *(Fig. 9.5)* are:

- A formal structure
- Task oriented
- Permanent
- Make a direct contribution to organisation's collective purpose
- Consciously organised

Informal groups are collections of individuals who become a group when members develop interdependencies and influence an individual's behaviour to meet a mutual need.

An organisation needs to assess the relationship between formal and informal groups and determine to what extent these hinder or enhance the organisation's ability to meet its business objectives.

5. Group Effectiveness

There are a number of variables that are likely to impact on the performance of a group of people. These are shown in *Fig. 9.6*, and each one of the elements has to be managed to ensure the desired performance is achieved.

	Informal Organisation	Formal Organisation
A. Structure		
(a) Origin	Spontaneous	Planned
(b) Rationale	Emotional	Rational
(c) Characteristics	Dynamic	Stable
B. Position Terminology	Role	Job
C. Goals	Member satisfaction	Profitability or service to society
D. Influence		
(a) Base	Personality	Position
(b) Type	Power	Authority
(c) Flow	Bottom up	Top down
E. Control Mechanism	Physical or social sanction (norms)	Threat of firing or demotion
F. Communication		
(a) Channels	Grapevine	Formal channels
(b) Networks	Poorly defined, cut across regular channels	Well defined, follows formal lines
G. Charting	Sociogram	Organisation chart
H. Miscellaneous		
(a) Individuals included	Only those "acceptable"	All individuals in work group
(b) Interpersonal relations	Arise spontaneously	Prescribed by job organisation
(c) Leadership role	Result of membership	Assigned by organisation
(d) Basis for interaction	Personal characteristics, status	Functional duties or position
(e) Basis for attachment	Cohesiveness	Loyalty

Fig. 9.5: The informal and formal organisations. From "Organizational Behaviour: Concepts and Applications", Jerry L. Gray and Frederick A. Starke (Charles E. Merrill, Columbus, Ohio, 1984).

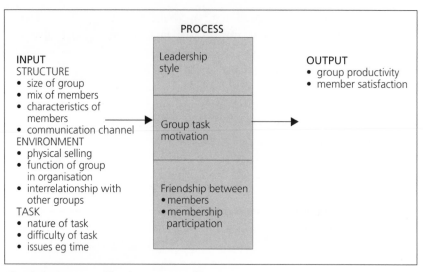

Fig. 9.6: Factors affecting group effectiveness

ANALYSING THE MANAGEMENT OF STAFF AND SKILLS

1. Types of Working Patterns

As society's motives change due to more disposable income and an increase in the need for greater leisure time, companies are having to find more creative ways of planning workloads. This requires focus on determining accurately, workloads and worktimes to complete particular tasks. A range of options exists for maximising workforce outputs. These include:

- Full time and part time staff – getting the right mix and proportion of full and part time staff to achieve the company goals.
- Use of external resources, such as consultants, subcontractors, etc.
- Use of technology – as a means of substituting human beings for repetitive tasks.
- Flexible hours – many organisations offer their employees a degree of flexibility in the hours that are actually worked by the people.
- Flexible working practices – dependent on the flexibility of the tasks and the ability of the individuals to undertake a greater range of activities.
- Overtime – to manage the abnormal workloads.

The working practices adopted in an organisation have to be reviewed for effectiveness and satisfaction on the part of the individuals.

2. Performance Indicators and Staff Appraisal System

These are the measures used by an organisation to evaluate the extent to which an individual or group of individuals meets the expectations and target set by the strategy. In addition, consideration is given to the system of collecting data and the degree to which the indicators are relevant and consistent with the organisation's objectives.

The performance indicators are inputs to the staff appraisal system. Usually this is done once or twice a year. The purpose of the system is to identify strengths and weaknesses in the individuals.

The assessment of the staff system should address the following issues:

- Type of system
- Reasons for having a staff appraisal system
- Factors taken into account in staff appraisal
- Does the system allow consistent measurement over a specific period of time?

3. Absenteeism

An analysis of the level of absenteeism within an organisation is generally a very good indicator of potential, and actual, problems that are likely to exist within an organisation. The analysis should explore not only the quantity of days lost, but also the seasonal trends and group trends that might exist. The reasons for the absenteeism need to be established and addressed.

Absenteeism is the outcome of an unacceptable combination of the factors listed above.

4. Reward Mechanisms

The assessment of reward systems should identify the strengths and weaknesses of the system of reward applied to the successful completion of a set of activities. These may comprise not only financial rewards, but also recognition leading to promotion, pensions, share options, and also other less quantifiable benefits such as cheap airline tickets for an airline employee.

The strategic appraisal has to define the type of system used and the positive and negative points of its implementation. Fairness to all employees needs to be explored, so that consistency exists across the whole organisation.

5. Recruitment Processes

The format for the selection of an individual to an organisation determines to a large extent whether an appropriate individual has been selected to deliver the needs of a strategy. The processes of selection and determination of the characteristics of the right candidate should be aligned with the strategic needs of an organisation.

In addition to the selection process, a cost is involved not only in the selection but also in terms of the salary to be paid and the flexibility to negotiate with a particular individual. Consideration also should be given to the settling in time that is needed for different individuals to acclimatise to different environments.

6. Job Design

One of the responsibilities of those who design the jobs is to look after the well-being of the staff. Taylor (ref. 9.2) suggested, in 1969, that one way of working based on scientific methods emphasised specialisation of tasks. However, some of the degree of repetition involved in this method can lead to health problems, such as stress. Emphasis should also be placed on ensuring that the activities entailed in a job definition do have some degree of completion. Badly designed jobs with no end sometimes lead to depression.

The characteristics of a well-designed job are:

* Skill variety
* Task identity
* Task significance
* Autonomy
* Feedback

Ref. 9.2: Taylor, F. W., "Principles of Scientific Management", (Harper, New York, 1971)

7. Relationship between Machine and Man in the Organisation

Different organisations manage the substitution of man and machine better than others.

Fig. 9.7 shows the characteristics of man and machines, and also the areas in which man is better than a machine, and vice versa. This assists the analyst in determining when it is most appropriate to employ a man or a machine in a business.

	MAN	MACHINE
Key features	• amass knowledge • draw upon knowledge when necessary • various thinking styles • prioritise • imagine • make and take decisions • interact verbally • extrapolate • invent • misunderstand • take risks • problem solving	• identical replication of actions • multiple replication of actions without error • continuous working over long periods • retain all facts • obey instructions fully
Activities performed better than the other	• operate outside basic instructions • make judgements • work reliably with incomplete information • compensate for disability • achieve similar ends by different means	• purely logical operations • achieve feats outside the range of human physiology

Fig. 9.7: A comparison of man and machine

SKILLS

Skills Assessment

The skills requirement is determined by the job roles and the strategy of the organisation. The key skills base can be laid out as shown in *Fig. 9.8*. The components of the skills base comprise each of the elements that are likely to impact on the strategy, such as:

- Project management
- Administration
- System design
- System analysis
- Engineering
- Legal
- Marketing, etc.

Fig. 9.8 can also highlight the current skills level, thus indicating the skills gap between the desired and actual levels of skills and capabilities of individuals.

Learning Methods and Training Processes

Five potential learning outcomes should be highlighted as part of any training programme. These are:

1 Intellectual skills
2 Cognitive strategies
3 Verbal information
4 Motor skills
5 Attitudes.

Skills base	Team members			
	A	B	C	D

Fig, 9.8: Skills analysis

Training is seen as the learning of behaviour and skills that are directed to achieving the organisation's goals and objectives. The emphasis of training is on the benefit to the organisation, though the individual does gain some benefit.

Training differs from education in that education is focused on broadening the knowledge and experience base of individuals themselves. Organisations need to determine, in line with the corporate philosophy, the mix of education and training which will best serve the company.

The systems employed and the cost associated with the development, linked to the outputs and how these are managed in an organisation, are critical to determining the adaptability and flexibility of the organisation to a rapidly changing environment.

Analytical Steps

Different levels of analysis are required depending on the size of the organisation. The larger organisation will have to depend on its individual managers and leaders to identify critical and exceptional trends that exist throughout the organisation. This has to form part of an overall monitoring system that forces the manager to consider the effectiveness of the "coaching" role of the manager and leaders. The analysis would be undertaken as follows:

LOWER LEVEL

1. Involve HR function to analyse the differences in individuals of the following:

    a   Motivation and drives
    b   Personality type
    c   Past experience
    d   Learning and education

2. Identify levels of compatibility between different individuals.

HIGHER LEVEL

3. List the different groups in the organisation, at the appropriate level and determine the factors most prevalent in the groups in terms of:

    a Sources of power
    b Social structure
    c Purpose of groups
    d Mix of formal and informal groups
    e Effectiveness of the groups

4. Identify the common themes that exist in the groups. These constitute the main inputs into the strategy development process.

5. Assess the management systems that are in place in terms of:

    a Working patterns
    b Performance indicators and staff appraisal systems
    c Reward mechanisms
    d Recruitment processes
    e Job design and job definition
    f Success of the man machine mix

6. Determine the strengths and weaknesses of each of the above
7. Assess the skills needs of the organisation.
8. Determine the current skills level.
9. Determine the skills gap in relation to the current strategy.
10. Identify and summarise the strengths and weaknesses of the staff and skills of the organisation using *Fig. 9.9*.

Factors	Description of current status	Strengths or weaknesses	Notes

Fig. 9.9: Summary table

Summary

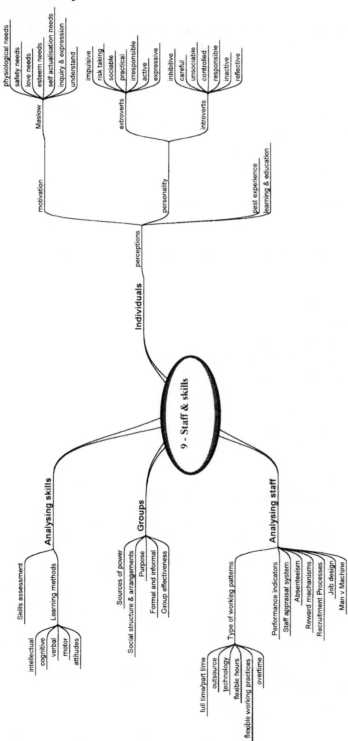

10

ORGANISATION STRUCTURES

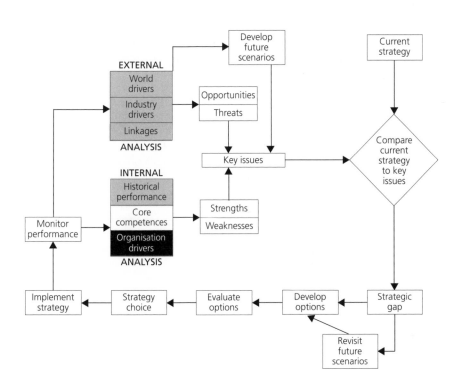

"The time is always right to do what is right."
Dr Martin Luther King Jr.

CONCEPTS

The organisation structure is the vehicle for the organisation to achieve its objectives in the most effective and efficient manner. An organisation structure allows the process of communication, authority and workflow to proceed through a formal arrangement of roles and relationships of people, so that the work is directed toward meeting the goals and accomplishing the mission of an organisation

This chapter looks at the holistic nature of the structure. In the next chapter we will look at the internal processes and linkages to identify strengths and weaknesses in the system.

To fully understand the advantages and disadvantages of an organisation structure, it is important, first, to appreciate the process of Organisation Design.

Organisational design is defined as:

> *"The systematic planning and creation of*
> *organisation structure, measurement and reward*
> *schemes, and personnel development programs to*
> *divide up the organisation's work while still achieving*
> *unified effort toward the organisation's goals."*

Lorsch and Lawrence (1967) defined the primary objectives of organisational design to be to:

- enable the company to deliver a product or service most effectively and efficiently given its strategic goals and desired market position.
- minimise any duplication of work.
- attain maximum flexibility within the organisation.
- maximise communications throughout the organisation.

Nitin Nohria (*Harvard Business Review*, 1991) highlighted the key issues that need to be addressed by organisation design as:

- The Division of Labour
  This involves the construction of teams, the sharing of activities in the most efficient manner.

- Co-ordination Mechanisms
  Ensuring all teams and members address the same issues.

- The Distribution of Decision Rights
  Effective and efficient decision making at all levels of the organisation.

- Organisational Boundaries
  Defining the limits of the organisation, and sub-organisations within, and defining responsibilities.

- The Informal Structure
  Encouraging the positive elements of informal groups.

- The Political Structure
  Encouraging the positive elements and differences in political power.

- The Legitimate Basis of Authority.

- Defining the Levels of Hierarchy.

The design of organisation structures tends to resemble preconceived theoretical models that the designers can relate to and understand simply. The advantage of designing structures based on theoretical models is that a basis for comparison and a prediction of response to different stimuli is provided. The theoretical systems are based on a number of different systems that designers are likely to interact with, such as:

1. Mechanical Systems

This type of system is based on principles of engineering and machines. It works very much on a response/reactive model. The structure places great emphasis on clarifying responsibility and authority with clear reporting lines. However, this type of structure tends to slow down decision making, and does not encourage creativity and rapid response to changing business environments.

2. Biological Systems

This system is based on nature and the achievement of balance in the environment. These structures encourage trust and openness, and a very democratic form of decision making. However, change in response to changing business dynamics is extremely slow due to the desire to involve large numbers of people in the decision making process.

Lorsch and Lawrence indicate that the inconsistencies caused by different models is due to the fact that mechanical and biological systems are long term systems, whose states are in equilibrium, and as such do not encourage flexibility and change, which is most definitely an important requirement in the current dynamic environment that businesses have to operate in. Therefore, the requirement is for a morphogenic system, i.e. one that can change its state, form or structure. This requirement for change is related to changing stakeholder expectations.

There is a need to produce a creative tension in the organisation where instability is continuous and the management skill is to make this positive.

Why Structure an Organisation?

Traditionally, whenever two or more people come together there have always been attempts to create a "formal" relationship, e.g. marriage, that clearly identifies individuals' responsibilities and the goals of the group, however informally. This need exists to enable individuals to better cope with the level of complexity that exists between the expectations and desires of different individuals.

Expectations and desires are different for each of the individuals due to the different environments that these individuals exist in. The question that arises is do we need to force a structure on a group of individuals? How would they develop without the stimulus from a third party, such as an "unskilled" manager?

Observing group behaviour shows that individuals, on an informal basis, will develop a natural role structure, where people are more conscious of their own objectives and those of the group as a whole, e.g. Parent and Teachers Associations. This tends to lead to greater commitment and responsibility.

Pressure due to poor performance occurs due to poor recruitment policy, not identifying the mindset of individuals and managing these mindsets. Instead, "unskilled" managers assume that the employees are incapable of thinking and do not need to know their objectives. This type of management can be termed "Monkey Management". The "unskilled" manager imposes artificial boundaries, which show the monkey manager in a position of unjustified power. However, the human leader creates an environment that allows the employee to reach the heights of his/her natural creativity.

Ideally, the structure should encourage creativity and foster a team spirit, and also allow consideration of the complexities of the business environment.

In a business context many variables and complexities exist that need to be managed and effectively integrated.

These are:

- Resources – human, financial, physical, etc.
- Geography – modern day business has taken on more global proportions and this needs to be managed
- Product – the tangible outcomes
- Skills – the amalgamation of different abilities
- Strategy.

However, the key criteria that will largely influence the design of an organisation's structure is the extent to which decision making will be decentralised or centralised and the extent to which processes and functions within the organisation are formal or informal *(See Fig. 10.1)*.

PROCESSES / DECISION MAKING	FORMAL	INFORMAL
CENTRALISED	Regimented	Entrepreneurial
DECENTRALISED	Delegative	Intrapreneurial

Fig, 10.1: Structure types

Combining these variables gives four types of structure:

Fig. 10.2 shows the advantages and disadvantages of centralised and decentralised systems.

	Benefits	Difficulties/Problems
Centralisation	• Ability to achieve and control consistent strategy • Co-ordination of activities • Simple control systems • Allocation of resources facilitated • Speedier strategic decision-making	• Failure to achieve response to local conditions • Difficulties in developing general management capabilities • Cumbersome and costly central overheads
Decentralisation	Operational • Rapid response to specific of local problems • Improved motivation/ commitment Strategic • When environmental or decision-making complexity too great to deal with at apex of the organisation	• Definition of split of operational and strategic responsibilities • Failure to devolve *power* of decision-making, resulting in: • Lengthy referral processes and delayed decisions • Frustrated management • Complicated control procedures

Fig. 10.2: Centralisation and decentralisation

The effectiveness of the different types of structure should be compared against three criteria *(Fig. 10.3)*. These are:

1. Responsiveness to Change
This is the speed at which the organisation can respond to the changing business environment.

2. Communication
This is the level and flow of information through all levels of the organisation, which is likely to affect decision making.

3. Distribution of Power
This is the perceived extent of power within the organisation.

The type of structure needed within an organisation is dependent on the development stage of the organisation *(Fig. 10.4)*, i.e. which stage of the lifecycle the organisation and the industry it operates are in.

	RESPONSE	COMMUNICATION	POWER
REGIMENTED	Slow	Good, but slow	Hierarchical
ENTREPRENEURIAL	Very slow	Poor	Ambiguous
DELEGATIVE	Medium	Fairly good	Autonomous
INTRAPRENEURIAL	Fast	Fast, but poor	Team

Fig. 10.3: Structure effectiveness

STAGE	STRATEGIC IMPERATIVE	TYPE OF STRUCTURE
Introduction/Growth	Market share	Entrepreneurial
Shake out/ Maturity	Cost efficiency	Regimented
Decline	Product development	Intrapreneurial

Fig. 10.4: Structure and lifecycle

The basic forms of organisational structure that are traditionally recognised are:

- Simple Structure, *Fig. 10.5*
- Functional Structure, *Fig. 10.6*
- Divisional Structure, *Fig. 10.7*
- Matrix Structure, *Fig. 10.8*
- Network Structure, *Fig. 10.9*

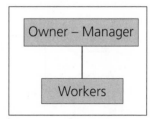

Fig. 10.5: Simple Structure

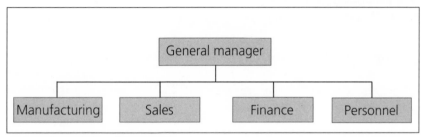

Fig. 10.6: Functional structure

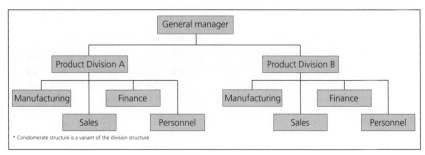

Fig. 10.7: Divisional structure

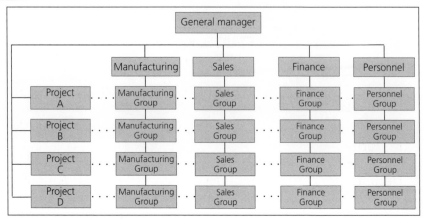

Fig. 10.8: Matrix structure

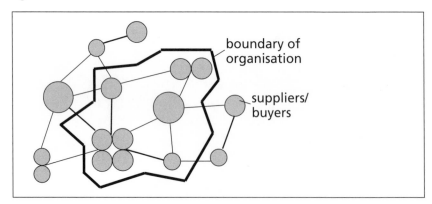

Fig. 10.9: Network structure

Fig. 10.11 shows descriptions of these different structures.

History of thinking on structure

Fig. 10.10 shows the history of the development of thoughts on structures.

Time	Founder	Thoughts	Key variables
1949	Fayol	Devised functional structure • ideal for single product • appropriate to all organisations Was he wrong?	Markets & products were early in PLC Company strategy was based on market development Simple business structure
1962	Chandler	Structure follows strategy Multi-unit business Decentralisation Managerial hierarchy essential	Global organisations Creativity in hands of few Managerial control vs leadership Low levels of competition
1963	Sloan	Responsible for growth in General Motors' global development Multi-product business Multi-divisional structure Federal plan Decentralisation	Low competition Regulated environment Growing markets Managerial control Market segmentation Complex business
1980s		Matrix management	Improved communication Multi-national corporations Geographical control Lower overheads: less duplication

Fig. 10.10: History of structures

Type	Description
Simple	No functions or product groups. Appropriate for small organisations. Usually dominated by owner. Employees are generalists
Functional	Specialised functions like Sales, Marketing, R&D, Finance etc. Appropriate for medium-sized organisations.
Divisional/ Holding Company	Standard functions designed around products, segments or territories. Appropriate for organisations serving many different markets with many products.
Matrix	Functional and Divisional areas are combined. Functions are permanent, projects are temporary. Appropriate where the external environment is complex.
Network	Builds on relationships between groups and individuals, both within and outside the organisation.

Right: Fig. 10.11: Description of different types of structure

Characteristics of different structures

Fig. 10.12 shows the relative advantages and disadvantages of different structures based on applying Nohria's criteria to each of the structure types.

	Functional	Divisional	Matrix	Network
Division of labour	By inputs	By outputs	By inputs & outputs	By knowledge
Co-ordination mechanisms	Hierarchical supervision, plans & procedures	Divisional General Manager & Corporate Staff	Dual reporting relationships	Cross-functional teams
Decision rights	High centralised	Separation of strategy & execution	Shared	Highly decentralised
Boundaries	Core/Periphery	Internal & external markets	Multiple interfaces	Porous & changing
Importance of informal structure	Low	Modest	Considerable	High
Politics	Inter-functional	Corporate-Division & Inter-Divisional	Along matrix dimensions	Shifting coalitions
Basis of authority	Positional & functional expertise	General management responsibility & resources	Negotiating skills & resources	Knowledge & resources
Resource efficiency	Excellent	Poor	Moderate	Good
Time efficiency	Poor	Good	Moderate	Excellent
Responsiveness	Poor	Moderate	Good	Excellent
Adaptability	Poor	Good	Moderate	Excellent
Accountability	Good	Excellent	Poor	Moderate
Environment for which best suited	Stable environment	Heterogeneous environments	Complex environment with multiple demands	Volatile environments
Strategy for which best suited	Focused/Low cost strategies	Diversified strategy	Responsiveness strategy	Innovation strategy

Fig. 10.12: Different structures – the relative advantages and disadvantages, from Nohria (HBR, 1991)

Structure in the 90s

The 1990s has seen the development of more flexible structures such as:

- Virtual organisation
- Learning organisation
- Trans-national organisation

All of the above are discussed later in this chapter.

Clearly, the changing environment, increasing dynamism and competition, has placed greater needs on organisations to be more responsive, adaptive and flexible. Organisations today need to be:

- Self sufficient
  Within the boundaries of the organisation's mission statement, it needs to be able to develop all necessary elements of the value chain.

- Self adjusting
  Based on automatic diagnostic processes, by combining feedback and control mechanisms, organisations can alter their paths with little intervention.

- Self maintaining
  Respond to changes by instigating adequate staff training etc. by identifying the gaps and taking corrective actions.

- Responsive to different national requirements
  Understanding the internal and external cultural differences.

- Integrated on a larger geographical base
  Global intention is the strategic imperative.

- Encouraging creativity by empowering individuals.

In summary, the organisation needs, more than ever, to develop synergistic value by harnessing the creative energies of individual team members and ensuring a *zanshin* (Japanese term meaning an on-going intuitive awareness) of the internal and external environments.

A fundamental criteria for this type of organisation is the formation of small, manageable, process-based teams that have specific roles within the framework of a larger corporate body. Smaller teams have many inherent benefits, largely due to the reduced chance of conflict that is likely to exist in larger groups. Also self-management becomes more prominent. Peters and Waterman in *In Search of Excellence* also allude to the fact that there was a loss of entrepreneurial capability in larger groups.

The driving force of these changing requirements is the development of information technology, hardware and software. Therefore, the key to managing organisations in today's environment is dependent on the successful integration of human resources and technology.

Some Organisational Solutions

Virtual Organisation

The virtual organisation uses technology to link people, assets and ideas in a temporary organisation. Key premises are:

- Excellence through partnerships and alliances

- Network links through technology

- Establishment of shared values between partners

- No boundaries of operation

- Creation of value added along the value system

- No hierarchy

- Total flexibility

- Decentralised decision making.

Key issues facing the virtual organisation are:

- Trust amongst managers

- Lack of control of certain functions. This can be tied in with process re-engineering.

One of the problems with the virtual organisation is that there is no infrastructure for implementing creativity in the broader sense.

Arguably, costs may be lower, though there is also a tendency for these to experience serious overrun, e.g. Eurotunnel, but do these outweigh economies of scale, experience curve effects and the infrastructure benefits that a good corporation would offer?

In terms of sustainable competitive advantage, would a small virtual corporation be able to create the breakpoints to gain the advantage?

The virtual organisation does offer greater flexibility and increased market responsiveness within the confines of its brief, but can it exist without a corporate entity which should ensure the future existence of the team members? Perhaps the role of the virtual organisation is more effective within the corporate environment.

Learning Organisations

The basic premise for the learning organisation is that the organisation cannot learn unless the individual members of an organisation are committed to learning.

Peter Senge (ref. 10.1) identified five disciplines as being essential for the development of a learning organisation. These are:

1. Systems Thinking
Management needs to move away from assuming linear relationships exist between a number of complex variables. It is essential that the relationship is understood in a systemic and holistic manner.

2. Personal Mastery
The growth of the learning organisation is dependent on an individual being objective and self managing, and gaining a desire to improve and develop their own skills base.

3. Mental Models
All parts of an organisation need to understand when and why generalisations and leaps of abstraction are made, which in turn will enable the creative element to flourish.

Ref. 10.1: Senge, P., "The Fifth Discipline", (Currency Books, 1990)

4. Building Shared Visions

The role of the leader is to ensure that there is a commitment, and not compliance, to a vision.

5. Team Learning

Though an organisation is made up of individuals, it is their performance in teams that actually drives or slows an organisation.

The learning organisation places great emphasis on the individual taking responsibility for his or her own development path. This also has implications on the role of the leader who needs to foster an environment that ensures personal and corporate responsibility. It is important for the individual to build an awareness of his needs, and be positively critical of gaps in capability.

The learning organisation emphasises the importance of changing and managing mindsets.

Some of the difficulties with this type of organisation are associated with shareholder pressure to deliver short term results. In addition, managers' attitudes need to be changed so they move away from being task managers to mindset managers. ICL is an example of an organisation implementing such a programme.

Trans-national Organisation

Formulated by Bartlett and Ghoshal (ref. 10.2), the Trans-national Organisation addresses the issues of global integration and national responsiveness. It is based on attaining a deeper understanding of the administrative heritage of the company. The administrative heritage represents the strengths an organisation has built up from its past.

Trans-nationals concentrate on building and expanding their strengths or strategic assets into sources of competitive advantage across a broader geographical base.

Bartlett and Ghoshal, therefore, conclude that trans-nationals compete on the basis of:

Ref. 10.2: Bartlett, C. A. and Ghoshal, S., "Managing Across Borders", (Century Business, 1992)

- Global efficiency
- National responsiveness
- The ability to innovate on a worldwide basis.

Networks

Networks focus on creating links with suppliers and buyers to increase the competitiveness of organisations, on similar lines to the virtual organisation. Some of the problems associated with networks are:

- Suppliers are encouraged to supply competitors
- Over dependence on one company can lead to reducing quality

If this type of organisation is the vision of the future, then how does it affect the nature of a company's business? The tendency will be to focus on distinctive capabilities (see Chapter 11).

Organisations will have to concentrate on building these capabilities to ensure a competitive advantage.

Analytical Steps

1. Describe the type of organisation structure.
2. What are its characteristics, as shown in Fig. 10.12?
3. Highlight in each of the boxes in Fig. 10.12, in black, the strengths of each of the attributes, as applied to your organisation.
4. Highlight in each of the boxes in Fig. 10.12, in red, the weaknesses of each of the attributes, as applied to your organisation.
5. Highlight and prioritise the key issues, strengths and weaknesses, facing your organisation, in terms of its structure.

Summary

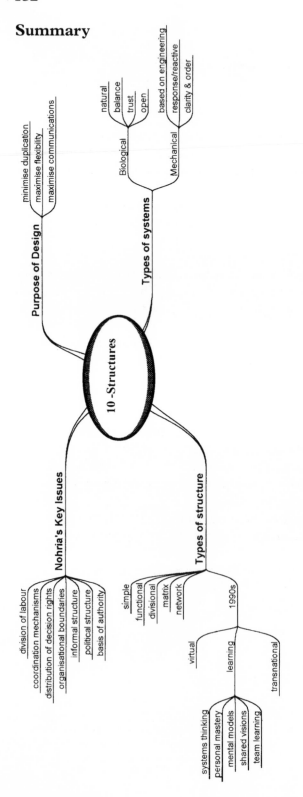

11

IDENTIFYING THE CORE
COMPETENCIES

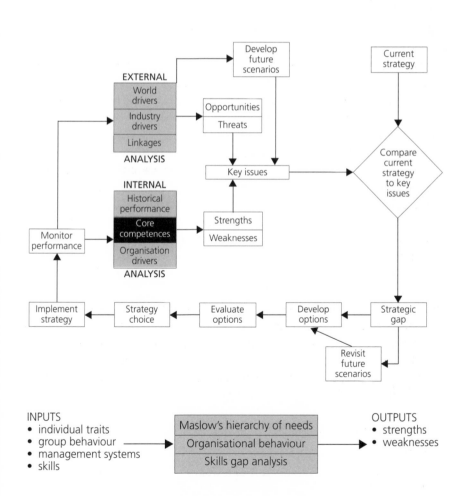

INPUTS
- individual traits
- group behaviour
- management systems
- skills

Maslow's hierarchy of needs
Organisational behaviour
Skills gap analysis

OUTPUTS
- strengths
- weaknesses

*"Everything as it exists in nature has one perfect
purpose. One should look for that one attribute that
makes it unique from all other things."*
Aristotle

CONCEPTS

Core Competencies and Distinctive Capabilities

All organisations possess strengths and weaknesses, and a key part
of any strategic analysis is to determine the internal strengths and
advantages that an organisation possesses. The internal perspective
of an organisation is key to developing a strategy that is appropriate
for a particular organisation.

There is little point in developing a strategy that fails to make optimal
use of the key strengths of an organisation, simply because an
opportunity exists. An opportunity can only be realised if the
organisation is capable of taking advantage of the opportunity.
Therefore, prior to developing strategy an organisation needs to
understand what its strengths and weaknesses are. More important,
the organisation needs to be able to articulate its key strengths, the
areas in which it is better than its competitors, that are difficult to
replicate. These strengths are defined as the **core competencies** of
the organisation. However, identifying the areas an organisation is
good at, better than its competition, and that are difficult to replicate
is not an easy task. Where can you identify areas in an organisation
that are difficult to copy? Where is the uniqueness of the organisation's
strengths? Yet all organisations possess the potential to have core
competencies.

John Kay (ref. 11.1) identified the term Distinctive Capabilities as
an alternative way of looking at some of the key strengths. Kay defined
Distinctive Capabilities as activities that allow organisations to
produce at lower cost than their competitors or to enhance the value
of their products or services. However, the difference is that distinctive
capabilities can be replicated, with sufficient investment.

Kay identified four areas as potential sources of distinctive
capabilities:

*Ref. 11.1: Kay, John, "Foundations of Corporate Success", (Oxford
University Press, 1993)*

1. Strategic Assets – Kay identified three types of strategic asset *(Fig. 11.1)*
2. Architecture – This is the network of relationships an organisation has with its many stakeholders *(Fig. 11.2)*
3. Innovation – This focuses on the process of using innovation as a culture within an organisation to gain competitive advantage.
4. Reputation – This concerns the process of building up reputations, maintaining and losing reputations.

The potential sources of advantage tend to be in very intangible parts of the business. They are not always easily identifiable and hence difficult to copy as far as the competition is concerned. The distinctive capabilities will have certain advantages and disadvantages *(Fig. 11.3)*.

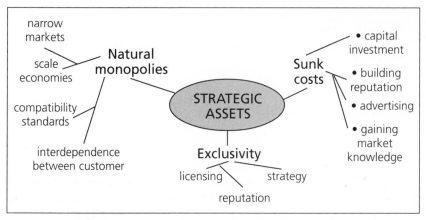

Fig. 11.1: Types of strategic assets

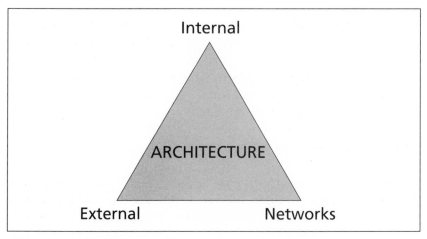

Fig. 11.2: Architecture

	Advantages	Disadvantages
Strategic assets		
Reputation		
Innovation		
Architecture		

Fig. 11.3: Assessing distinctive capabilities

Defining Value Added

One of the key premises of the core competency is that it should add value to the business activity of the organisation. There would be little point in developing core competencies in areas that failed to add value to the business. Value Added can be defined as increases in appropriate perceived benefits to the various stakeholders of a business.

In terms of identifying core competencies it makes sense to consider, at the same time, the impact on the value added to a business. Porter (ref. 11.2) developed a tool to enable the strategist to make this assessment, called Value Chain Analysis. Value Chain Analysis considers the relationship of all activities within an organisation to determine the sources of advantage.

Value Chain Analysis

Porter (ref. 11.2) suggested that all businesses have a continuous flow of activity in their business. Citing the example of a manufacturing business, he identified its following key activities:

Ref. 11.2: Porter, M., "Competitive Advantage", (The Free Press, 1985)

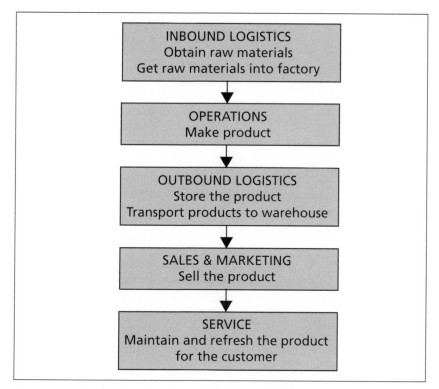

Fig 11.4: Key activities of a manufacturing company

These activities he called PRIMARY or CORE activities. Primary activities are activities that exist in their own right. They are activities that can be "hived off" or outsourced to other organisations. Primary activities, in essence, are businesses in their own right.

For a service industry it is unlikely the flow of activity will include inbound and outbound logistics. In some businesses, such as consulting, sales and marketing may be the first activity. It is important that you "personalise" the flow of activity to reflect your business as it stands at the moment.

An issue arises as to whether this flow of activity provides the customer with the most value added, in which case the flow of activity needs to be re-engineered, hence 'Business Re-engineering'. The notion of business re-engineering comes from the value chain, with emphasis on the core activities, and support functions being inherent within the core parts of the business.

Within an organisation there are three areas that need to be managed. These are:

1 People
2 Information and Technology Development
3 Money

However, these activities are inherent within the primary activities of the organisation, and do not exist in their own right, which is why they are shown as dotted lines on *Fig. 11.5*. Thus, the management of these three areas is called SECONDARY activities, defined as Human Resource Development, Technology Development and Procurement, respectively.

Across the whole organisation is the head office functions, or firm infrastructure, of the organisation, such as strategic planning, financial planning, and other policy making functions within the organisation.

Within the value adding activities of the organisation there are some areas that are more difficult for competitors to replicate than others. Predominantly, there are two areas that could represent major sources of advantage that would be difficult to replicate *(see Fig. 11.5)*. These are:

1 The connection between the support activities and the primary activities (shown as boxes 2-4, 6-8, 10-12, 14-16, 18-20), and
2 The linkages between the various primary activities (shown as a, b, c, d).

The more intangible the competency, the more difficult it is to replicate.

The margin (box 22) represents the value added to the company through additional pricing on top of the cost that the customer is prepared to pay for. This also represents a key part of the analysis, enabling an understanding of the boundaries of the business. If the overall value chain has an upper limit in terms of the margin, say, then the organisation is "forced" to rethink its processes, in order to make them more efficient and effective.

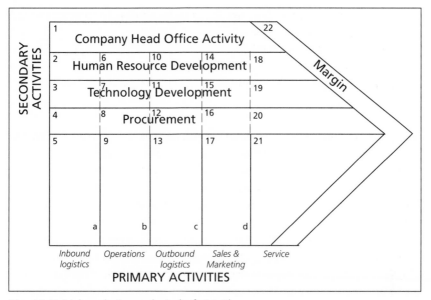

Fig. 11.5: Value chain analysis (ref. 11.2)

The value chain analysis is used to identify the strengths and weaknesses, in relation to each box. In addition, an organisation can highlight the box which is most likely to create a unique advantage in its environment. Consequently, the strategy might concentrate on building this competency.

Key Success Factors (KSFs)

KSFs are the critical activities a business needs to undertake to be successful. The identification of these factors depends on the knowledge of the customers, suppliers, competitors and all other stakeholders. A combination of the core competency focused on addressing the issues related to KSFs will ensure long term sustainable advantage.

Key Success Factors can also be defined as what it takes to be successful in business.

Developing Core Competencies and Capabilities

An organisation might consider it has little or no competencies, currently. However, the organisation feels, as part of its strategy, that it needs to develop a core competency. Value chain analysis will enable the strategist to focus on the area that is likely to generate the greatest impact. Industry analysis, combined with customer surveys, will identify the Key Success Factors of the business. The organisation needs to take these KSFs and establish how an advantage can be created within its own framework. This then forms the basis for the strategy.

The key to creating advantage lies in keeping the strategy simple and developing the areas that will generate the greatest value. These areas tend to be those concerned with people and culture.

The question arises, why do the boxes stated represent a possible core competency? The combining of the support and primary activities, successfully depends on the "glue" that will make these activities appear seamless. This "glue" is the most difficult area to define, to control and, therefore, to replicate. The "glue" is the culture and systems that unify these processes.

Many organisations have a tendency to outsource some of these secondary activities, most notably technology development, in particular, information technology and systems. Unfortunately, organisations are "giving" a potential competency to an outside organisation, which will most likely sell this competency to competitors. Some surveys have suggested that as many as 85% of organisations are looking for outsourcing this support activity. The reason – IGNORANCE, and a lack of comfort with the technology.

Activity 8

Describe the activities, in terms of the value chain, for an NHS Trust provider.

Solution to Activity 8

Primary activities:
As a service provider, an NHS Trust provider does not follow the manufacturing model. However, taking the provision of treatment as the transformation process, the following definitions of the model could be adopted:

- Inbound logistics – the activities which govern the scheduling and admission of patients (e.g waiting list management, clinic management).

- Outbound logistics – locations where treatment is provided (acute hospitals, community clinics, and GP surgeries, patient's homes etc.)

- Operations –provision of clinical services and directly related activities (e.g surgery, nursing, pharmacy, Professions Allied to Medicine [PAM]).

- Marketing – activities related to internal market contracting (contracting, costing, negotiations). Also income generation through peripheral activities to provide additional resources for operational activity.

- Service – activities in support of operational areas. Includes clinical correspondence from Trust consultants to referring GPs, medical training and patient caring.

Secondary activities:
These fit the model in a more conventional manner:

- Procurement – the purchase and provision of materials and services, including locum services, (could also be considered an HR activity).

- HR – recruiting and training of staff, particularly junior doctors on rotation. (Training medical staff is also identified as a Service activity.)

- Technical development – medical advances are important to the provision of good medical care. However, the better use of information is vital to making best use of resources. Key activities in this field are the development and implementation of Clinical Information (CIS) and Management Information (MIS) Systems.

- Infrastructure – a Trust must place emphasis on quality improvements using clinical and general audits to provide evidence of system controls and to identify areas for improvement.

Core competencies are necessarily those which provide the patient with treatment, and are key to the patient experience, i.e. the management of waiting and admission, the provision of treatment, and managing the locations at which treatment is provided.

Competitive advantage
An NHS Trust provider has the ability to treat a patient across the whole range of locations and the full spectrum of treatments. The range of locations available where treatment can be provided allows a Trust to provide services near to the patients, where appropriate. This is attractive to patients and thus popular with GPs who actually pay for the procedures.

Government policy has recently moved towards a more primary (i.e. GP) led health service, with less emphasis on secondary care in Acute units. A Trust is well placed to respond to this policy shift, or any future reversal, by adjusting the balance of services. The Acute or Community units are much less able to adapt to such changes without major changes.

The design of buildings is geared to support the flow of activity, which reduces costs associated with moving patients around the hospital while also improving the experience for the patients.

Vulnerabilities
Within a Trust's activities, a major weakness can be the marketing function. While the contracting process is vital to a Trust's income, it is supported by a team heavily involved in the process.

Human Resources are vital to the operation of a Trust, as are junior doctors. Yet recruiting medical and nursing staff is becoming increasingly difficult as there is a reported shortage of doctors overall, despite increasing student numbers, which has meant that many doctors at Registrar level find it more lucrative to sign on as a locum, rather than taking a contract with a Trust.

	Inbound logistics	Operations	Outbound logistics	Marketing	Service
Trust infrastructure	Clinical service Improvement Programme (CSIP) for continual improvement of quality. Use of clinical and general audit to provide evidence of system controls.				
Human Resources	Staff training Rostering	Medical recruiting Professional training	Multi-skilling Recruiting Training	Recruiting	Control of aggression training Customer relations training Complaints process
Technical development	Clinical Information System Management Information System Ergonomics	Clinical Information System Management Information System Ergonomics Clinical audit	Ergonomics Clinical Information System Management Information System	Internet Intranet	Building management systems CHP
Procurement	IT	Consumable Locums Equipment Energy IT	Equipment Transport Clinical services	IT Communications	Services Equipment Supplies IT
	Waiting list management Clinic management Pre-admission clinics Patient transport management A&E triage	Treatments • Mental health • Surgery • Medical • Nursing • PAM Diagnostic services • Pathology • Radiology Pharmacy	Acute hospitals Short-stay/day surgery units Day hospitals Community clinics Respite/long-term care hospitals Community staff • GP surgeries • Patients' homes Tertiary referrals	Contracting Costing Income generation Negotiation	Clinical staff training Clinical correspondence Patient catering Maintenance Car parking provision
	Inbound logistics	Operations	Outbound logistics	Marketing	Service

Areas of core competence

Fig. 11.5a: Value chain of an NHS Trust provider

Non-medical recruiting can also be difficult at senior levels since the salaries a Trust can offer are significantly lower than those in the commercial sector. Combined with repeated attacks on NHS managers by politicians and the press over the past few years, it is difficult to attract and retain high quality staff.

A Trust's key linkage to any external organisation is through the local GPs, and may be weak. Despite the vital role of a GP, whether a fundholder or not, in determining a Trust's activities, there is often little involvement of GPs in the planning process. It is hoped that this will change for the better in the future.

Analytical Steps

1. Identify the flow of activity in your organisation. Clearly, this will differ for different companies and different industries.
2. Consider the three key elements to be managed within the core activities:
   a Money or cash – PROCUREMENT
   b People – HUMAN RESOURCE DEVELOPMENT
   c Technology – TECHNOLOGY DEVELOPMENT
3. Construct the matrix showing your value chain *(see Fig. 11.5)*.
4. Consider each of the boxes in the value chain and describe the activities your organisation undertakes in respect of that box.
5. Mark, in black, all the strengths of the organisation in relation to each of the numbered boxes.
6. Mark, in red, all of the weaknesses of the organisation in relation to each of the numbered boxes.
7. Review the strengths and drill down to identify the core competencies.
8. Consider, through market research, what the value chain looks like for your competitors.
9. Consider what the ideal value chain might look like from your customers' perspective.
10. Locate on the value chain the box representing the key success factor in your business, based on earlier research.
11. Identify internal strategic responses to focus on your strengths and divert away from the weaknesses or overcome your weaknesses.

Summary

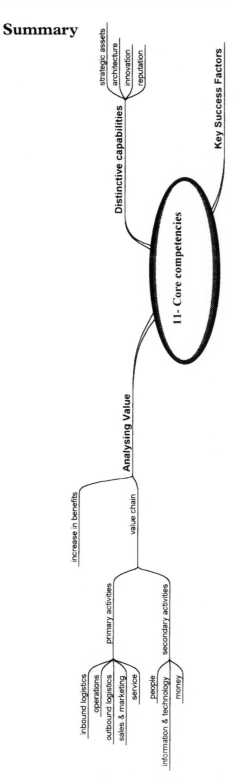

12

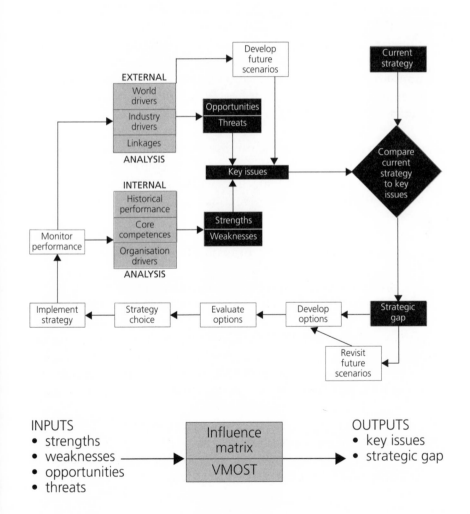

INPUTS
- strengths
- weaknesses
- opportunities
- threats

Influence matrix

VMOST

OUTPUTS
- key issues
- strategic gap

"Never mistake motion for action."
Ernest Hemingway

CONCEPTS

On completion of the external and internal analyses, a basis for decision making is present. No organisation can tackle all the issues it is facing, and therefore has to prioritise the most important issues the strategy has to address. These priorities are likely to vary depending upon the perspective being held by the respective group of decision makers involved.

Many forms of ranking can be used to prioritise. The key issues can be summarised in the form of a SWOT analysis. The SWOT analysis is a situation audit. It describes the environment in terms of its position today as a balancing of the internal strengths and weaknesses, with the external opportunities and threats. The external factors can be summarised as opportunities and threats, while the strengths and weaknesses are internal. Factors such as "improve costs" are not opportunities, but are weaknesses, today.

The decision makers have to determine which strengths, weaknesses, and opportunities and threats are going to become the focus of the future strategy. Different perspectives will want to focus on different issues depending on their backgrounds.

The influence matrix, as used in the scenario appraisal *(Fig. 13.2)*, is a useful tool to help with the prioritisation process.

Each of the variables, that have been identified, in the analysis of the current situation form the elements of the complex and dynamic system that is the organisation. These can be compared with each other to determine, through the Influence matrix, the most significant issues that should be addressed by the strategy. However, be aware that if the analysis is too general and not sufficiently rigorous, the factors will be difficult to assess, and thus the strategy will be vague.

The prioritisation process is a negotiation process, and different groups at different times may identify different factors. Thoroughness is gained through the discussion process, which also encourages an exploration of why different stakeholders may have different priorities.

Defining the Current Strategy of the Organisation

The current strategy can be articulated using VMOST.

VMOST is used to help determine the consistency and alignment of the strategy to its various components.

The key questions that need to be asked in this part of the analysis are:

VISION

- To what extent is there a vision?
- How clear is this vision?
- Who owns the vision?
- Is the vision well communicated and shared by key people in the organisation?
- Is the vision emotional and engaging?
- Is the vision distant, yet achievable?
- Is the vision ambitious and stretching?

MISSION

- Is there an explicit mission in the organisation or is there an implied mission?
- Is the mission actually a mission or is it a goal?
- Is the mission appropriate and relevant for the vision and the environment?
- What is the purpose of the mission? Is it for staff motivation or for PR purposes? Is it successful?
- Does the mission provide a realistic view, from the management's perspective, of the capabilities of the organisation?
- Does the mission express the policies and values of the organisation? Do these tie in with the actual values identified in the analysis of the culture? Are the policies valid and relevant to the environment?
- Where does the mission fit in *Fig. 1.2*? What are the advantages and disadvantages of this?

OBJECTIVES

- Are these SMART? (SPECIFIC, MEASURABLE, ACHIEVABLE, RELEVANT, TIMEBOUND).
- Do the objectives help fulfil the mission?

STRATEGY

- What are the basic elements of the strategy?
- How effectively is the strategy being implemented?
- To what extent does the current strategy address the issues that have been earlier prioritised from the analysis?
- Is the strategy relevant and appropriate?

TACTICS

- How is the strategy being carried forward on a day to day basis?
- Do the tactics reflect the aims of the strategy?
- Are the tactics coordinated between different parts of the organisation?
- Are the tactics being monitored for success?

You need to consider if all five elements are aligned with each other, for consistency.

It is important always to question why we are doing this analysis. This will help you focus on the issues. VMOST enables us to see whether there is any strategic logic in what the company is doing and whether it is being implemented in the right way and in a consistent manner.

Activity 9

Assess the following VMOST for a listed UK-based software company.

Mission Statement:
The company's mission statement is "To be a leading pan-European multi-vendor IT services provider".

Objectives:
- Revenues of £250m by year 2000.
- To become a major provider of IT solutions in European countries.
- To be a leading UK IT service provider.
- To increase the value of stock to stockholders.

Strategy:
- Strong external growth through aggressive acquisition strategy, primarily in Europe.
- Strong internal (organic) growth through highly-motivated sales team and customer retention through quality of service.
- Increased investment in marketing and activity and promotion of the brand name.
- Expansion and diversification of product offerings.
- Capitalise on inherent rapid growth of the European IT market.
- Capitalise on the technological changes in the computer services industry by providing a single source for high-end solutions to information systems problems.
- Emphasis on service solutions as opposed to product-related business.

Tactics:
- Acquisition of IT service companies who can complement existing product offerings as well as broaden the current range. Resultant acquisitions would also increase the client base in UK and Europe.
- Integration of companies in order to capitalise on operational and cost efficiencies.
- Capturing of valuable skills/knowledge through selective acquisitions. The current skills shortage in the market is cause for concern as the IT industry is dependent on high numbers of skilled staff.
- Promotion of 'partnership' ideology with clients' internal IT departments to deliver service on their behalf. Building such relationships is likely to develop loyalty with the client as long as you are providing a good service.
- Diversification of product offerings, primarily through company acquisition.
- Capitalisation of year 2000 opportunities.
- Capitalisation on the introduction of the Euro.

- Expansion of the share option scheme to wider range of employees. This has been instigated to engender a 'sense of belonging' to the company by employees with the hope of retention of skill levels within the company.
- Share offering on Nasdaq & Easdaq markets to raise capital for next stage of acquisition policy/
- Reductions in numbers of contract staff to reduce operational costs.
- Generation of approved supplier list to benefit from approved supplier discounts.
- Development of IT infrastructure.

Issues Gap

Comparison of the current strategy with the key issues facing the organisation enables the strategist to determine the extent to which the current strategy needs to change to address the issues it is facing. The strategy team needs to discuss and explore which issues should be focused on and the degree to which the strategy should change. Bear in mind that the analysis does not provide answers. If anything, it probably raises more questions than answers, but it is key in the decision making process. The personal and intuitive input of members of the strategy team is a vital ingredient in the strategic analysis process.

The strategy will also have to decide which of the key issues are critical to success of the strategy, i.e. which of these are the Key Success Factors.

Stakeholder Requirements

Using the earlier framework of stakeholder analysis, determine the forces supporting or forces against the current strategy. These forces represent the issues that need to be addressed to ensure the smooth implementation of any strategy.

Solution to Activity 9

VISION	
• To what extent is there a vision?	None
• How clear is this vision?	N/A
• Who owns the vision?	N/A
• Is the vision well communicated and shared by key people in the organisation?	N/A
• Is the vision distant, yet achievable?	N/A
• Is the vision ambitious and stretching?	N/A

MISSION	
• Is there an explicit mission for the organisation, or is there an implied mission?	Explicit mission exists
• Is the mission actually a mission or is it a goal?	Mission is stated as a goal
• Is the mission appropriate and relevant for the vision and the environment?	Not clear
• What is the purpose of the mission? Is it for staff motivation or for PR purposes? Is it successful?	Not clear
• Does the mission provide a realistic view, from the management's perspective, of the capabilities of the organisation?	No
• Does the mission express the policies and values of the organisation? Do these tie in with the actual values identified in the analysis of the culture? Are the policies valid and relevant to the environment?	No

OBJECTIVES	
Are these:	
• Specific	One out of four
• Measurable	Yes
• Achievable	Yes
• Relevant	Yes
• Timebound	One out of four

STRATEGY	
• What are the basic elements of the strategy?	Growth by acquisition
• How effectively is the strategy being implemented?	Unknown
• To what extent does the current strategy address the issues?	Not very clearly
• Is the strategy relevant and appropriate?	The statement lacks clarity on how a strategy will be used to take advantage of the opportunities

TACTICS	
• How is the strategy being carried forward on a day-to-day basis?	Not clear from the statement
• Do the tactics reflect the aims of the strategy?	Yes
• Are the tactics co-ordinated between different parts of the organisation?	They appear to be, but not totally clear
• Are the tactics being monitored for success?	Not known

> **Overall assessment of VMOST**
> No real vision or inspiration behind the strategy. Unclear strategy with little discussion on values and the mode of operation. Statement appears to exist for artificial rather than a functional purpose. Probably ineffective at the organisational level.

Analytical Steps

1 Complete SWOT analysis.
2 Identify top strengths, weaknesses, opportunities and threats.
3 State the current strategy in terms of VMOST.
4 Compare the emphasis of the current strategy with the key issues identified in 2 above.
5 State the gap between 2 and 4 above.

Summary

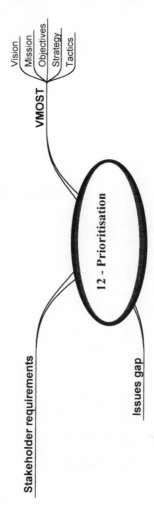

13

CREATING SCENARIOS FOR THE FUTURE

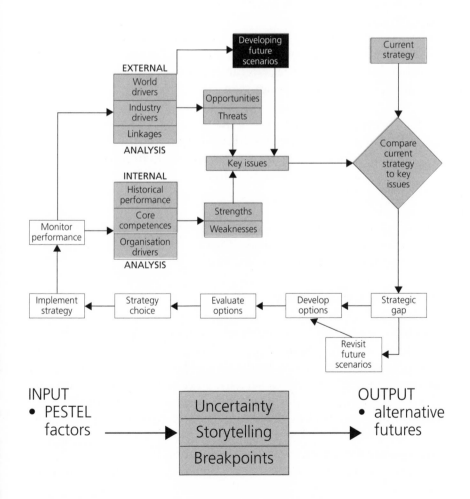

INPUT
• PESTEL
factors

Uncertainty
Storytelling
Breakpoints

OUTPUT
• alternative
futures

"Courage is the result when fear meets faith."
Unknown

CONCEPTS

What is a scenario?

A scenario is a possible future that has a realistic probability of occurrence. In the process of developing the future strategy, an organisation should attempt to predict the future and consider the possibilities. This establishes a frame of reference in which to place the organisation. Scenarios ensure that an organisation develops a strategy that is relevant to the environment in which it exists. Scenarios help the strategists to broaden their horizons and avoid addressing issues that are too narrow.

Scenario development starts with a picture of the future, which is held by the strategy team and its members. This picture needs to be translated into actions that attempt to address these pictures. The key factors in scenario development are:

- The deployment of a more qualitative approach as opposed to using econometric based modelling
- The creation of a view of the external environment, so that the organisation can cope with market changes in the long term future.

The long term view requires the strategist to have a detailed understanding of the dynamics of the business and its environment. Assumptions need to be fully justified.

Assessing Uncertainty

Scenarios are the result of uncertainty that exists in the environment in which an organisation operates. The more uncertain an environment, the more diverse the possible futures. The more certain the environment, the more scenarios begin to converge into one possible outcome. Therefore, the level of uncertainty in an environment needs to be determined prior to developing scenarios.

An organisation exists as part of a very complex environment, and as such is represented by a system comprising the major drivers or

PESTEL factors of the environment *(Fig. 13.1)*. Each of these factors interacts with each other to differing degrees, thus influencing the future outcomes of the environment, including the internal parts of the organisation.

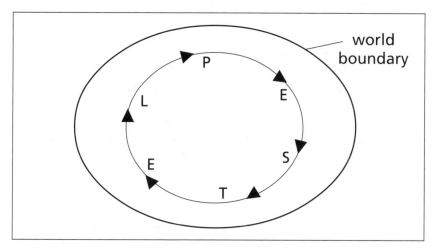

Fig. 13.1: Interactive nature of the external environment

Uncertainty, according to Johnson and Scholes (ref. 13.1), is a function of two elements:

1. Dynamism – this relates to each of the individual variables that comprise the environment. Dynamism is a function of:
- the rate of change, and
- the magnitude of change of each variable.

The rate of change of a variable is the frequency with which change in the variable has occurred, historically. Consideration needs to be taken of the trends and their likely impact at different points in the future.

The magnitude of change of a variable is the degree of change of each variable, i.e. how much has it changed by, when it does change?

2. Complexity – this relates to the environment as a whole, and is a function of the:
a Interconnectivity of all variables making up the system, and
b Knowledge of the dynamics of the system

Ref. 13.1: Johnson & Scholes, "Exploring Corporate Strategy", (Prentice Hall International)

The interconnectivity of the variables in the environment can be determined by constructing an influence matrix *(Fig. 13.2)*. The size of the matrix represents the number of variables that comprise the environmental system. Each of the variables is replicated as columns and rows. These are represented by A, B, C, D, for example, in *Fig. 13.2*. The influence matrix has two purposes:

1   *To determine the most influential variable of the system as a whole.* This is similar to the crowbar effect, ie. minimum effort for maximum impact. This key variable should become the core theme of the scenarios.
2   *To determine the level of interconnectivity of the variables.* This helps determine the relationships between the variables and their connections. The more interconnectedness of the variables, the more complex the environment, and the more diverse the possible futures.

Starting at box 1 *(Fig. 13.2)*, the analyst asks the question "To what extent does variable A influence variable B?" The response will be one of the following:

0 – no link
1 – weak link
2 – strong link

The relevant number is inserted in the appropriate box. Next (box 2) consider "To what extent does A influence C?", and this continues until the whole matrix is complete.

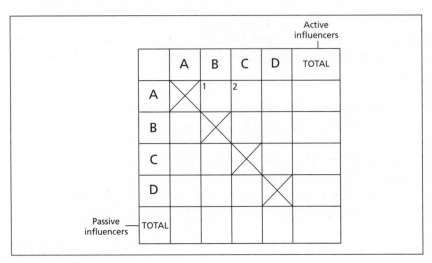

Fig. 13.2: Influence matrix

The greater the number of 2s, the greater the level of inter-connectivity. The greater the number of 0s, the simpler the system. Adding the total of all columns and rows gives the active and passive influencers.

The active influencers are the key drivers of the system. These usually are the variables that need to be focused on in terms of scenarios and hence, the strategy. Note that the numbers associated with the matrix are meaningless on their own. Their value is to provide an indication in comparison with other variables.

Passive influencers are the variables that are most likely to change or be affected by the system.

Knowledge is required to make an educated guess at the future direction of the environment. The degree of knowledge required will vary from system to system.

An example of the application of the influence matrix might be as shown for the tourist hotel industry in *fig. 13.3*.

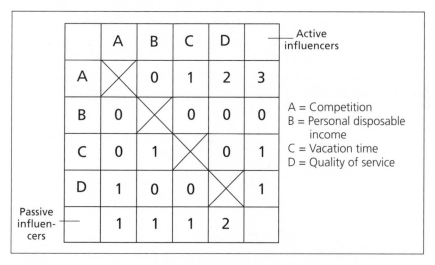

	A	B	C	D		Active influencers
A		0	1	2	3	
B	0		0	0	0	A = Competition
C	0	1		0	1	B = Personal disposable income
D	1	0	0		1	C = Vacation time
Passive influencers	1	1	1	2		D = Quality of service

Fig. 13.3: Applying the influence matrix to the tourist hotel industry

Though some of the scores are open to debate, the analysis shows the following points:

a Key active influencer is the competition for this system
b The variable that is most heavily influenced by the system is the quality of service

c   The low range of scores suggests there is little
    interconnectivity in the system that is shown.

Developing Scenarios

The first stage of developing scenarios is to agree the timescales of
the strategy. There is a danger that the same scenarios will be
developed whether we say one, three or five years! This is a result of
the tendency to treat the future as a point, as opposed to a variable
over different periods of time. The timing of the scenarios needs to
be thought out in terms of the level of dynamism of each of the
variables.

There are three levels of scenario. *Fig. 13.4* shows that the broad
PESTEL factors are projected into future scenarios of the world
within which the organisation operates. These scenarios are cascaded
down to the industry level, thus giving a view of the external
environment. At the company level, we will develop options to address
the scenarios that we have projected. This ultimately will lead to the
strategy of the organisation.

Developing scenarios encourages strategists to think outside the
traditional and accepted boundaries. Earlier discussions on
breakpoints provide a useful input into this process. For each of the
key influencers consider the potential breakpoints and changes in
trends that can have a major impact, or require a major change in

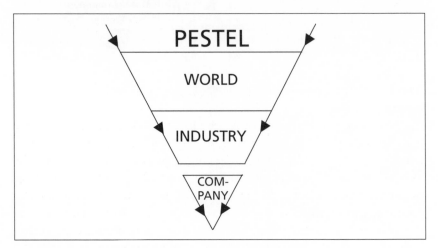

Fig. 13.4: Levels of scenarios

strategic direction. On many occasions there may be changes in the environment that have no history today, ie. they are unlikely to be picked up by the analyses.

Brainstorming, through word association, can highlight radical changes that will totally change the context of the business environment. This may also highlight a direction that would allow the company to create a breakpoint for its own advantage. Some of the recent changes in the area of technology and IT demonstrate the effectiveness of this approach.

The strategists will also want to determine the variables and assumptions about the future that they can and cannot change. Identify the triggers that will warn of the prospective changes.

The key to success in this exercise is having the mindset that everything, and anything, is possible. In addition, the team needs to be encouraged to make mental leaps and not only think about incremental differences in the future. Take to extremes, both negatively and positively, the Key Success Factors and assumptions made about the business that are appropriate today. Assume that a KSF today becomes totally irrelevant in 20 years' time.

Story Telling to Describe a Scenario

The future is like a blank sheet of paper. The more depth in description of the scenario, the greater the understanding of the future and the greater likelihood of clarity in the strategy. The scenario needs to be described like a story. It needs to create a fullness in description.

The key to making a scenario work in an organisation is the ability to communicate the story effectively. It needs to be able to engage the senses of the team, stirring the emotions so that the issues are highlighted. Much has been written, in 1998, about the benefits of corporate story telling within strategic plans, as opposed to the extensive use of bullet points, which tend to get lost in large organisations. There are some valid points, but equally the communication should not be just the written word. However, in the context of scenarios, the written word can be quite powerful. You also want to ensure that everyone in the organisation gets the same picture of the future, and that there is no room for confusion.

The senses that need to be engaged are:

- smell
- sight
- hearing
- touch
- taste

There are many advantages in using a story or fictional writer to articulate the scenario. These people are creative and understand how to engage the senses.

How Many Scenarios?

It is important to limit the number of alternatives that are actually explored, as this can create more confusion than is desired. "Worst case/best case" type scenarios should also be avoided as this polarises the view of the strategy team which can be quite detrimental to the organisation.

The number of scenarios should be an even number to avoid taking the middle ground. Remember that the development of the scenarios does not suggest a definitive outcome, but a range of possible outcomes. There is an inherent danger that if too many scenarios are created then focus on central issues is lost and a type of paralysis sets in. Though this is a creative exercise, the scenarios should reflect realistic outcomes as opposed to remotely likely outcomes.

One of the scenarios should represent the most likely, and also the most desired, by the key stakeholders in an organisation.

Using Scenarios

Scenarios do not let the organisation predict one future. They force the organisation to think of the possibilities, and as best as possible, prepare strategies that will allow adaptation of the original strategy when necessary. Scenarios also ensure that the relevant variables in the environment are monitored by the organisation. *Fig. 13.5* shows the possible application of scenarios. A, B, C, D are alternative futures. The company decided to pursue a strategy following scenario A. However, monitoring of key variables suggests that scenario C is more likely after a period of time into the strategy. The organisation

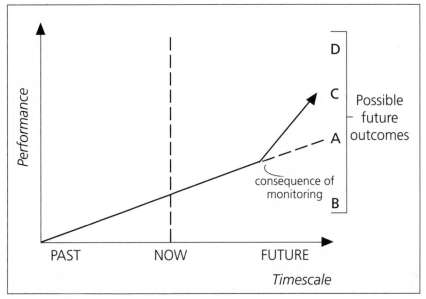

Fig. 13.5: Using scenarios

has decided to shift its strategy, as it has built in contingencies within its original strategy, to take account of the changing environment.

Benefits of Scenario Planning

The key benefits of this process are:

- Forces the strategy team to adopt an external view of strategy
- Creates a long term perspective of business by identifying what is important
- Provides insight into the dynamics of the business environment
- Articulates the assumptions within a strategy for better understanding within the organisation
- Generates novel and innovative ideas
- Forces the strategy team to look at sensitivity issues
- Provides the basis for contingency plans
- Provides an early warning system by focusing on key indicators.

Dangers of Scenario Planning

Many organisations talk of scenarios in the same context as strategic options. Options are possible solutions to scenarios. The organisation should aim to create scenarios first and use this as an input to creating options, otherwise the tendency is to make the scenarios fit the options, which defeats the purpose of the exercise. Maybe separate teams should be employed in the two exercises.

Outline Scenarios: an example

The following example shows a possible application of the concept to Ghana and the air transport industry in Ghana.

Scenarios are developed on the following basis:

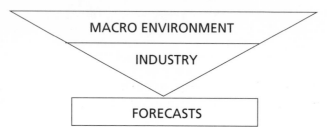

The key macro issues that have been identified as the major influences of the future are:

- GDP growth is the major influence that will drive the economy
- GDP growth per head is critical to meet the government's objective of becoming a middle income country
- the share of agriculture to industry needs to change, which will increase the growth in urban areas
- the level of private savings and investment needs to improve quite radically.

Two scenarios have been considered purely for this illustration. These are:

OPTIMISTIC – the optimistic scenario is represented by the Government's Vision 2020 strategy document. Though very admirable in its aims, it is felt from an analysis of the current trends that the achievement of Vision 2020 is indeed optimistic. Ghana manages to exploit its reputation for stability and lack of corruption

---

to form a focus for West Africa trade. The economy grows at a rate which will lead it to becoming a middle income country, following an accelerated growth model. The macro environment is managed so well that substantial foreign investment begins to grow significantly.

PESSIMISTIC – this assumes that certain elements worsen to their worst case. In some cases the current situation and trends also represent the worst case. This scenario also considers an unstable and undemocratic government following popular discontent with the lack of progress being made under a more democratic regime.

FACTOR	OPTIMISTIC	CURRENT LEVEL	PESSIMISTIC
Political framework	Open democratic	Current	Undemocratic & unstable
GDP growth rate	8%	5%	4%
level of private investment (%GDP)	26%	19%	10%
level of private saving (% GDP)	18%	8%	5%
inflation	5%	50%	80%
GDP per head (US$)	525	445	350
GDP per sector			
- agriculture	18%	46%	55%
- industry	37%	16%	12%
- services	45%	38%	33%
weather	benign	continues as is	drought similar to 70s80s
number of state-owned enterprises	minimal	130	300
population growth rate	2%	3%	3%
relationship with neighbours	stable	stable	poor
rate of urban growth	6%	4%	3%

The key elements to be considered for the macro environment scenarios are:

Air transport scenarios

Optimistic case
- Growth in economy and macro environment leads to 15% growth per annum in travel which exceeds the Boeing forecast for intra African and Europe-Africa growth of 7.7% and 4.9% respectively.
- Additional growth is largely as a result of increasing confidence with Ghana as the West African hub. There is increasing diversion of traffic from Lagos and Abidijan to Accra.
- The fuel tax is reduced from the current level of 38% to a comparable level of other West African countries.
- Facilities and service levels at Accra are perceived to be significantly better than at other African airports.
- Procedures for gaining entry visas are relaxed and significant hotel development occurs, thus encouraging increased tourism.
- Frequency of flights improve on a daily basis to key trading partner countries, with better managed flight timings, encouraging increased business travel.
- Fares are reduced to comparable levels of other countries.
- Airline is privatised, thus allowing an increase in the number of relationships with larger airlines, improving connections and access to new markets.
- Airspace is liberalised, allowing greater competition in both domestic and regional markets.
- The number of free trade zones is increased, particularly around the international airports.
- Storage and transportation facilities, particularly warehousing, cold storage, and air cargo are developed to allow for growth in trade.

Optimistic case – The Story

Martin Smith, the CEO, permitted himself the luxury of a smile as he lowered the report he had just finished reading, sat back in his chair and looked out of his office window at the hustle and bustle that was now Accra International Airport. A perfect clear blue sky that seemed to stretch forever, mirrored the endless opportunities that were suddenly opening up to him. Although he would never have admitted it, Martin had not dared to believe that the situation could have become so positive so quickly.

The privatisation of the airline had led, as he'd always known it would, to an increase in the number of relationships with larger airlines, improving connections and access to new markets. Fares had been reduced and the liberalisation of airspace had led to greater competition in both domestic and regional markets. The increase in tourism and it's knock-on effects, had come as no surprise – he had known that procedures for gaining entry visas were to be relaxed and that significant investment was going into hotel development. However, the figures included in the report exceeded his – and others' – expectations. Boeing had forecast a growth per annum in travel of 4.9% for Europe-Africa and 7.7% for intra-Africa. What a wonderful shock, then, when growth in the economy and macro environments, caused by increasing confidence with Ghana as the West African hub, resulted in 15% growth – almost double that predicted! The reduction in fuel tax, from 38% to a level comparable with other West African countries, had been another important factor, and the increase in the number of free trade zones, particularly around the international airports, led to another significant piece of the jigsaw being fitted into place. Now it made absolute sense to gear up for growth in trade – and storage and transportation facilities, especially warehousing, cold storage and air cargo, were being developed.

Martin stood up and walked to the window. The airport, it seemed to him, was a microcosm of the changes being felt throughout the country. There was a sense of optimism and enthusiasm – the very real beginnings of a 'can-do' culture. A plane taxied into place on the runway. Martin watched it, transfixed, as if it was a sight he had never seen before. As the plane began to pick up speed, Martin's smile returned, developing into a deep laugh. Now right now! – it really was true to say that, in more ways than one, Ghana was taking off! Martin watched the plane disappear into the endless blue sky and returned to his desk. What a beautiful day!

Pessimistic case
- Airline becomes a vehicle for the military and becomes isolated from the world markets.
- Travel growth slows down to less than 3% per annum.

- Domestic services are discouraged and limited to key routes for military purposes.
- Hotel and infrastructure development is halted.
- Current procedures for gaining entry into Ghana are increased.
- Fuel taxes are maintained at current levels.

Pessimistic case – The Story

Martin Smith, CEO, shook his head in quiet disbelief as he lowered the report he had just finished reading, sat back in his chair and looked out of his office window at the seemingly deserted buildings of Accra International Airport. How absurd, he thought, calling this an international airport when there are more clouds in the African sky than there are planes on our runways!

Martin drummed his fingers on the desktop. Had he really been so filled with ambition, enthusiasm and certainty when he first sat behind this desk? Or had that been a different man? One who did not know the meaning of the word 'defeat'. One who had never been confronted by such sorry statistics and predictions as those contained in the report he had just read.

Since he had taken over as CEO, Martin's vision of a successful, bustling airport had been shattered by a sequence of events that had moved with an irresistible force and inevitable consequences. Procedures for gaining entry into Ghana had been increased and, consequently, travel growth had slowed to less than 3% and hotel and infrastructure development had been halted. Fuel taxes had been maintained and an isolated 'Ghana Airways' had become a vehicle for the military, with domestic services discouraged.

Martin pushed the report to one side of his desk and took out the gold-nibbed fountain pen that had been a birthday present from his wife. 'Use this to write or sign only the most important documents,' she had said. And now he was going to. It was time for Martin Smith to resign.

These scenarios can be translated into workable forecasts.

Forecasts
Optimistic

Year	International passengers	Growth	Domestic passengers	Growth	Total	Growth
1986	340944		65407		406351	
1987	266175	-22%	38776	-41%	304951	-25%
1988	251074	-6%	33114	-15%	284188	-7%
1989	298767	19%	20839	-37%	319606	12%
1990	306477	3%	5782	-72%	312259	-2%
1991	362281	18%	2020	-65%	364301	17%
1992	306593	-15%	9205	356%	315798	-13%
1993	313967	2%	10376	13%	324343	3%
1994	352103	12%	13200	27%	365303	13%
1995	368202	5%	18050	37%	386252	6%
1996	402608	9%	22068	22%	424676	10%
1997	450921	12%	28688	30%	479609	13%
1998	518559	15%	37295	30%	555854	16%
1999	596343	15%	48483	30%	644826	16%
2000	685794	15%	63028	30%	748823	16%
2001	788664	15%	81937	30%	870601	16%
2002	906963	15%	106518	30%	1013481	16%
2003	1043008	15%	138473	30%	1181481	17%
2004	1199459	15%	180015	30%	1379474	17%
2005	1379378	15%	234020	30%	1613398	17%
2006	1586284	15%	304266	30%	1890510	17%
2007	1824227	15%	395494	30%	2219721	17%
2008	2097861	15%	514142	30%	2612003	18%
2009	2412540	15%	668385	30%	3080925	18%
2010	2774421	15%	868900	30%	3643321	18%
2011	3190584	15%	1129570	30%	4320154	19%
2012	3669172	15%	1468441	30%	5137613	19%
2013	4219547	15%	1908974	30%	6128521	19%
2014	4852479	15%	2481666	30%	7334145	20%
2015	5580351	15%	3226166	30%	8806517	20%

Pessimistic

Year	International passengers	Growth	Domestic passengers	Growth	Total	Growth
1986	340944		65407		406351	
1987	266175	-22%	38776	-41%	304951	-25%
1988	251074	-6%	33114	-15%	284188	-7%
1989	298767	19%	20839	-37%	319606	12%
1990	306477	3%	5782	-72%	312259	-2%
1991	362281	18%	2020	-65%	364301	17%
1992	306593	-15%	9205	356%	315798	-13%
1993	313967	2%	10376	13%	324343	3%
1994	352103	12%	13200	27%	365303	13%
1995	368202	5%	18050	37%	386252	6%
1996	402608	9%	22068	22%	424676	10%
1997	414686	3%	22730	3%	437416	3%
1998	427127	3%	23412	3%	450539	3%
1999	439941	3%	24114	3%	464055	3%
2000	453139	3%	24838	3%	477977	3%
2001	466733	3%	25583	3%	492316	3%
2002	480735	3%	26350	3%	507085	3%
2003	495157	3%	27141	3%	522298	3%
2004	510012	3%	27955	3%	537967	3%
2005	525312	3%	28794	3%	551406	3%
2006	541071	3%	29658	3%	570729	3%
2007	557304	3%	30547	3%	587851	3%
2008	574023	3%	31464	3%	605486	3%
2009	591243	3%	32408	3%	623651	3%
2010	608981	3%	33380	3%	642361	3%
2011	627250	3%	34381	3%	661631	3%
2012	646068	3%	35413	3%	681480	3%
2013	665450	3%	36475	3%	701925	3%
2014	685413	3%	37569	3%	722982	3%
2015	705976	3%	38696	3%	744672	3%

Analytical Steps

1. Identify the key variables of the environment, using the earlier PESTEL analysis.
2. Assess the dynamism of each of the variables comprising the system.
3. Assess the complexity of the system as a whole by completing the influence matrix.
4. Determine the key influencers of the system.
5. Creatively identify the direction of the future based on the key influencers.
6. Create the scenarios.
7. Tell the story.
8. Translate scenarios into forecasts.

Summary

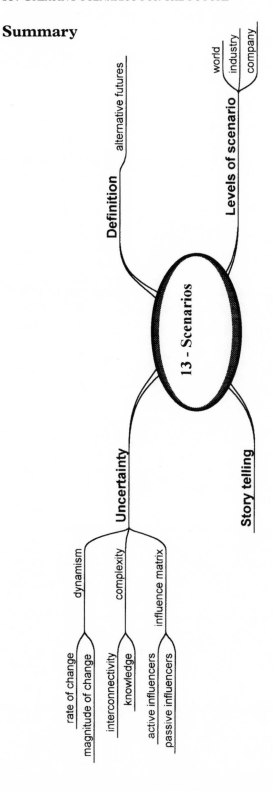

Section D

THE WAY FORWARD

14

CREATING OPTIONS

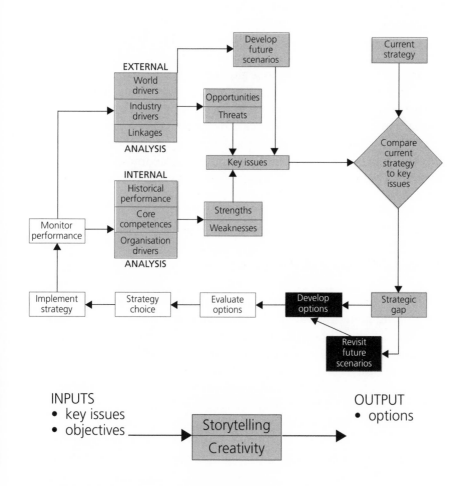

"Only an organisation with an excellent leader, which is able to conduct intelligence with superiority and cleverness,
Is certain to win,
This is the essence of strategy."
Sun Tzu

CONCEPTS

Theoretical Approaches

A number of academics and high profile business people have put forward their views on strategies and the areas of focus should follow a company to create strategic advantage. These approaches are generally based on empirical evidence gathered from observing good practice. The theoretical approaches provide a useful understanding of the approaches adopted, but that is all. The key to a successful strategy is **creativity**, and this is the major source of advantage for an organisation competing in a global marketplace. There is a huge danger that many organisations adopt approaches in reverse, from empirical evidence, rather than adopting strategies that fundamentally address the issues. These approaches form a cohesive part of the strategy, but they are part of a unique and complex picture that needs to be treated in a unique manner at all times. By attempting to adopt a blanket approach, a risk exists that inappropriate directions are taken.

Some of the most popular theoretical approaches are:

Porter's Generic Strategies

Michael Porter considered that companies needed to focus on developing generic strategies – strategies that had universal appeal throughout the organisation. These were like the philosophies of operation. He identified four possible strategic approaches *(Fig. 14.1)*. Porter identified two possible sources of creating advantage:

1. Low cost – A strategy concentrating on being one of the lowest cost players, which can yield above average returns despite competitive forces in the market. Porter considers the main requirements for achieving this position are:

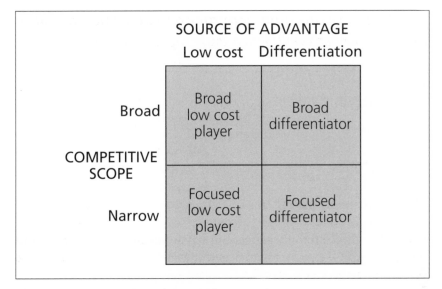

Figure 14.1: Porter's generic strategies

- Economies of scale
- Organisational learning
- Capacity utilisation

He suggests that the key to sustaining this competitive advantage is through utilising a combination of drivers and not relying on one single element.

2. Differentiation – A strategy concentrating on adding value to the product or service in such a way that distinguishes it from the competition, so much so that the customer is prepared to pay a higher price for the service. Differentiation can take many forms, but generally focuses on higher quality.

In addition, he identified that an advantage could be created by the competitive scope, i.e. did the company compete in a broad or narrow market, arguing that being more focused in a smaller market could create potential for differentiation. Adopting a FOCUS strategy concentrates on serving a narrow segment scope within an industry to the exclusion of others.

Mathur's Generic Strategies

Mathur (1988) develops the generic strategy of differentiation further by focusing on merchandise and customer support *(Fig. 14.2)*.

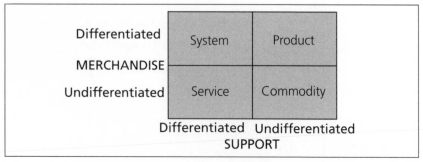

Fig. 14.2: Mathur's generic strategies

Mathur's support matrix identifies four types of support in terms of personalisation and levels of expertise *(Fig.14.3)*. In terms of merchandise Mathur identifies the key elements as "content" and "image", *(Fig. 14.4)*. Combining the variations yields 16 possible generic strategies *(Fig. 14.5)*.

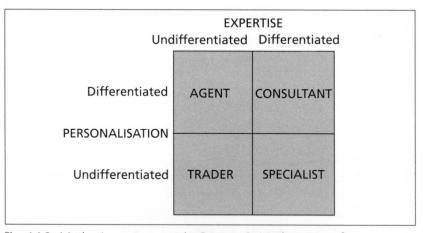

Fig. 14.3: Mathur's support matrix. Source: S. Mathur, 'How firms compete', The Journal of General Management, Autumn 1988.

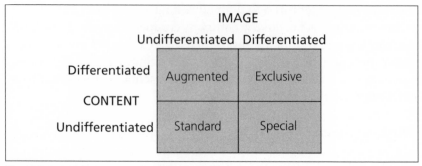

Fig. 14.4: Mathur's merchandise matrix

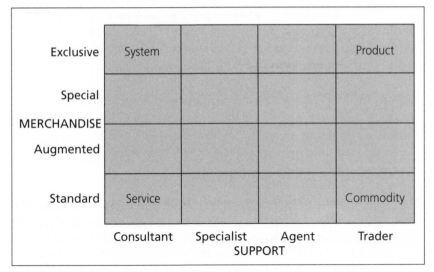

Fig. 14.5: Mathur's 16 generic strategies

Ansoff's Matrix

Igor Ansoff identified that the basis for strategic advantage lay in the options that arose from combining the product and market mix. He identified seven possible options as shown in *Fig. 14.6.*

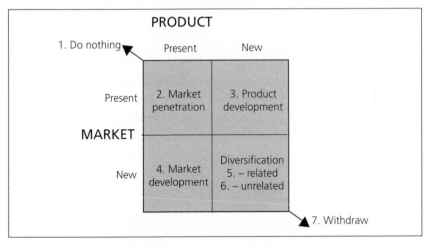

Fig. 14.6: Ansoff's growth vector components

1. Do Nothing – This essentially entails carrying on as the organisation has been with no changes to approach. A decision to do nothing does need to be taken.

2. Market Penetration – The objective is to gain market share for the current mix of product and market by undertaking activities such as improving quality, productivity or increased marketing, and generally involves the organisation in being more aggressive.

3. Product Development – This strategy involves building on the organisation's current knowledge and skills to develop new products within the existing market. Drivers for such a strategy include changing customer needs. High risks are involved in terms of pioneering costs and demand uncertainty.

4. Market Development – This approach is based on venturing into new markets with the current product or service. This could include entering new segments as well as increasing the geographical scope.

5. Related Diversification – This involves moving into a new area of business, but within the existing industry that is served. Advantage is gained through the benefits of synergy.

6. Unrelated Diversification – Involves development beyond the present industry into areas where there is no apparent relationship to current business.

7. Withdrawal – This is the decision to pull out of business altogether.

Ohmae's Competitive Strategies

Kenichi Ohmae, a strategy consultant with McKinseys, came up with options that were less theoretical, but more tactical. His approach was very much based on the Japanese philosophy of not taking the competition head on, until you are absolutely certain of winning *(Fig. 14.7)*.

Ohmae's definition of strategy is:

> *" the way a corporation endeavours to differentiate itself positively from competitors using relative competitive strengths to better satisfy customer needs".*

Competition is a key element when developing a strategy.

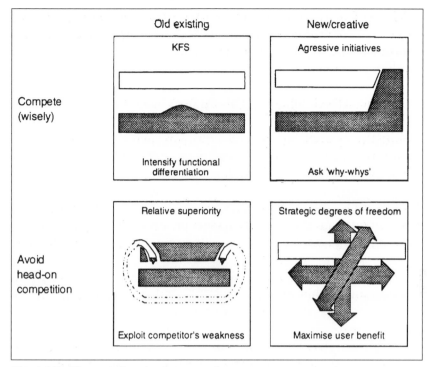

Fig. 14.7: Ohmae's four basic strategies

The four main strategies he suggests are:

1. Intensify functional differentiation – This strategy involves identifying the Key Factors for Success within the business and then ensuring that the organisation is better in this area than any of the competition. The strategy is based on the organisation's capability to increase market share and profitability. Critical to success is the ability to identify the key areas.

2. Exploit competitor's weaknesses – Based on understanding the competition's weaknesses and strengths, but then exploiting the weaknesses, using the organisation's own strengths, to gain benefit. A thorough understanding of the core competencies of the organisation is essential to success.

3. Ask "why – whys" – This approach is based on challenging the accepted assumptions of a business with a view to changing the rules of the business. This may involve changes in production technology or more innovative initiatives to the norm.

4. Maximise user benefit – Involves the development of innovations such as new markets or products. Creative inputs are essential to securing a lead for the organisation.

THE ESSENCE OF STRATEGY

Creativity and Options Development

In today's highly competitive environment, success is the result of creativity and its application to generating options. There is a tendency for organisations to adopt "me too" type strategies where their actions and approaches become so predictable that they cause the competition little discomfort. Much of this may be due to the fact that planning methods incorporating competitor analysis and benchmarking tend to foster imitation, rather than providing an opportunity to learn from another organisation's experience.

Organisations and strategists tend to favour the well-documented approaches of Porter, Ohmae, Mathur and Ansoff (see above) when looking at the options to take. Each of these approaches is built on a philosophy or a particular way of thinking. Porter's generic strategies focus on the concept of value; Ansoff's approach is built on the combination of product and market; Mathur's options focus on merchandise and support; and Ohmae's strategies are based on the Japanese treatment of competition, based on never "taking the enemy head on".

The identification of the issues resulting from the strategic analysis should be used as an input for non-linear thinking, an opportunity to create a difference. It provides the rationale for the process, but is not the driver for the development of strategic options. This is the realm of non-linear thinking or creativity. The creation of scenarios encourages a focus on new or emerging opportunities, on shifting the current way of thinking, rather than just exploring incremental developments from the current position. In a dynamic environment the need is for quantum leaps, in both thinking and action, to create a sustainable advantage.

The development of options should ensure that the process is not carried out in the abstract, but that the line managers are in control of the development process, as they are closest to the issues facing the organisation. The line managers are also responsible for the implementation of the strategies, which is where the majority of strategies fail. There has been a tendency in the past to isolate the strategic planning and implementation phases, thus creating the potential for blockages to success. In essence, the range of options is limited only by the creativity of the mind.

From the very outset, the strategy team needs to have a picture of the kind of organisation it sees as being necessary for the type of environment it operates in. This image may be the result of observing "excellent" companies or may be the result of the leader's personal desires. As stated in Chapter 1, in a dynamic, complex environment the organisation needs to be like water, moving from opportunity to opportunity as they arise, possessing the flexibility to change track quickly and in a timely fashion.

Just as a sports team can prepare itself for a well-known opponent, who may be a champion, organisations are able to compete more effectively when the competition is well known and the external environment is fairly stable. As more young, unknown athletes appear from new nations, that were previously not in existence, the probability of "shocks" occurring increases. The key for organisations dealing in an environment full of unknowns is to focus on being the best they can. This calls for greater focus on developing more internally based strategies rather than externally based approaches.

What is a Strategy?

From the very outset, our description of strategy helps us understand what we are trying to achieve and do, in the process of developing options. The characteristics of a strategy include the following:

Timescales
The strategy statement should reflect the desired position at a given point in the future. The timescales should be fully tied in with the overall strategic planning process. This should also take into account strategies that might be introduced at a later stage in the lifetime of an organisation.

Philosophy
This incorporates the attitudes and values that need to be instilled within an environment, and the beliefs that will gain commitment from the participants. The philosophy should also include a set of

guidelines to aid decision making. Philosophy can be expressed through a description of the vision and mission.

Actions
The strategy statement needs to articulate the external and internal, in the short, medium and long terms, actions that will make the strategy live.

Goals and Objectives
A clear statement of the aims of the organisation

Levels of Strategy

Strategy is essentially thought of in terms of three levels:

1 Corporate – This encompasses the approach to doing business adopted by the organisation.
2 Business Unit – Cascading down to more specific products and markets.
3 Operation – Direct management of the inputs and outputs to deliver the desired goals.

Understanding the variables that make up a strategy

During the process of creating options, the strategy team should explore, creatively, the possibilities of all variables that could make up the final strategy. There are no written rules as to what can and cannot be addressed in terms of the strategy, only our assumptions. In fact, the variables are represented by all of the issues that are likely to have been raised during the analysis part of the process.

Regardless of the emphasis required, every organisation's aim should be to follow the advice of Henry T. Ford who said companies need "to focus on delivering the best product or service it can, at the lowest cost, paying its staff as much as possible".

The variety of parameters that can form part of a strategy to deliver the above include the following:

1. FINANCE
Based on:
- Cost
- Shareholder value
- Revenue growth

The major focus of organisations should be to address not only the issues of reducing cost, but also whether the cost incurred needs to be incurred in the first place, i.e. are there assumptions being made about the activities being undertaken? Clearly, cost reduction strategies should form part of the overall strategy, and not be the only driver. After all, it is very easy to keep the costs down by getting rid of everyone! However, there is little long-termism and sustainability in that approach. Many organisations focus on cost as a primary driver, to the detriment of the quality of product or service on offer. Perhaps the ideal way of focusing on cost reduction is always to test whether the activities being undertaken are entirely relevant. This requires non-linear thinking, which might involve bringing people outside the organisation into the strategic planning process.

Many commercial organisations have shareholder value as a primary driver. Clearly, the shareholders are a major stakeholder, but some strategic decisions can, potentially, be taken without due consideration being given to important business issues, in preference to shareholder concerns. An organisation needs to build into its strategy its approach of coping with the demands and needs of the shareholders. There may be an education process that needs to be undertaken or the organisation may just simply have to take into account the views of the shareholders in determining its future strategy. In a society dominated by institutional investors, the objectives of some shareholders, such as maximising the financial returns in the shortest term, may not mirror the longer term goals of an organisation's management.

Simultaneously, the organisation also needs to explore realistic and relevant targets for revenue growth. The key word here is realistic. There are many examples of organisations that have been regularly achieving, say, 4-5% growth and assuming, in the following year, that they can increase this growth to 10-15%! This is not to suggest that this is not possible, but only if the fundamental assumptions behind the business, and the dynamics of that business, change totally. All the regular assumptions about how the business works have to be challenged, with new ways found to access the market for this increase. Many organisations are fearful of making such radical changes, leaving it to the point when it is too late. Faith is required, and clarity, in the implementation plan of the programme. The strategy needs to build in the changes that are going to be required to achieve the projected growth targets. Consideration also needs to be given to the timing of growth changes. Unrealistic assumptions about the time required to achieve abnormal changes to a trend are often made, reflecting the lack of understanding of the dynamics of the underlying system, of which the organisation is a part. The importance of this point should not be underestimated, as one of the most common reasons for the failure of strategy is the loss of faith when targets are not met.

2. INTERNAL PROCESSES AND STRUCTURE
Based on:
- Innovation
- Use of technology
- Values/image/culture
- Value added

The current trend, in an era of globalisation, is the creation of small companies that form part of a larger network. These smaller units create greater empowerment and increased flexibility to respond to changing environments. One of the major sources of advantage for an organisation is to build the ability to exploit innovation. The pace of change in technology is phenomenal and this is forcing companies to rethink their whole approach to gaining strategic advantage. The key to this is the ability to build flexibility in the organisation. Organisations such as ABB, formerly headed by Percy Barnevik, and Richard Branson's Virgin Group are examples of companies structured in such a way. The typical size of responsible business units is between 50 and 70 employees. This approach, which is built around relevant processes, necessitates a different skills mix in the staff. Greater all round capability is required so that positions within the organisation are more interchangeable and consequently there is less reliance on particular individuals.

An analogy might be to compare this form of organisation to the Dutch football team of the Johann Cruyff period in the 1970s. This team was dubbed the team of Total Football. The team was built around players who were not positional specialists, but skilful ball players who could play in a series of positions. This meant that at any time you might find the full back acting as striker. The full back would not try to get back into his original position, but stay where he was. The closest player to the full back position on the field would occupy the position, until the relevant change could be made.

In a business the football analogy is the equivalent to having functional specialists who carry out specific tasks without any real interest in other functions, hence possessing a limited view of the organisation as a whole. A very narrow perspective results, with a high degree of power being retained by the specialists. Conflict can be created because team members become very emotionally attached to their functions, as opposed to being attached to the organisation as a whole. People need to have a broader picture of the business world.

The whole basis for Business Process Re-engineering was the challenging of the traditional methods employed in an organisation. The structure of the organisation needs to have the flexibility within it to allow the changes to come from within, almost seamlessly. The culture of the organisation also should reflect the type of environment sought.

To be successful in global environments, the purpose of organisations is to promote cultural diversity, recognising regional interests and taking account of cultural differences. An organisation should aim to produce higher and higher quality goods and services, at the same time trying to reduce costs as much as possible. The organisation has also to assist employees with the opportunities to realise their aspirations within the working environment.

Within the spectrum of the strategy the organisation needs to take account of the desired image it wants to project. In today's society, values and social responsibility, along with ethics, are just as likely to form the cornerstone of a strategy as the product or service being offered. Whether these do form the cornerstone is irrelevant, but they should be given consideration within a range of possible options.

3. GROWTH
Based on:
* Learning
* People development
* Creativity

The only way any organisation will achieve sustained competitive advantage is through the development of its people. This is sometimes given secondary consideration, and organisations then wonder why no degree of sustainability was achieved. The environment within the organisation needs to be conducive to learning and personal growth, through performance appraisal methods and the other core elements of the strategy. It is probably fair to say that gone are the days when loyalty could be achieved through a good financial package. In the current environment, people want greater satisfaction and personal growth than they have done before, reflecting the needs of a more demanding and better informed society.

In the *Fifth Discipline*, Peter Senge talks in terms of individuals taking responsibility for their own development within an organisational context. He stresses the need to focus on five elements to create a flexible and adaptable learning organisation, where the individuals develop their creativity. The five elements have been discussed previously in chapter 10.

Corporate strategies should take the above into account.

4. CUSTOMER
Based on:
- Price
- Product
- Service
- Customer relationships
- Suppliers
- Distributors
- Competitors
- Geography

Customers are becoming more sophisticated and more demanding. They want shorter lead times for new products and greater service. More specific demands need to be met for smaller groups leading to greater detail for smaller groups.

Over the last few years there has tended to be a shift in the expectations of customers. They seek more benefit from what they are buying. Traditionally, customers expected a product or service, and that was it. Nowadays, the customer is seeking a more worthwhile experience, which is limited only by the imagination of the corporate world. This also offers a greater opportunity for increased revenue and greater customer loyalty. Organisations need to broaden out their offering and see how a more memorable experience can be achieved. Take, for example, the development of birthday cake making. Previously, customers went from buying ingredients for a cake, to buying a ready made cake, to actually buying a party, as offered by the likes of Discovery Zone, where the cake is just one element of the party or service.

The core emphasis on strategy development is to tie customers in on a long term basis, through combining unique features of a service. This requires exploring the possibilities and possessing a good understanding of the requirements of the customer, thus tailoring the product/service directly to the customer need. Involving customers in the decision making process and in the creation of an experience helps in increasing the loyalty. Part of this may also involve an organisation bypassing its lines of distribution, e.g. loyalty programmes in airlines, bypassing travel agents. A constant emphasis on delivering the best product or service at the lowest cost also increases the customer links.

The various categories above correspond to the categories used by Kaplan and Norton in the Balanced Scorecard (see Chapter 17).

HELP!

Greater flexibility is created by what can be called the HELP organisation. The HELP organisation is:

H – Horizontal
E – Empowered
L – Learning
P – Project based

As a horizontally structured organisation, decision making will be in the hands of the line managers and will be more responsive to the needs of the changing environment. More people are going to be involved in the strategy development process, suggesting greater buy-in at all levels. A flatter structure suggests organisations comprising collections of smaller teams, forming a more powerful network.

Greater empowerment to take decisions makes for greater flexibility. Passing full decision making responsibility to individuals, within a corporate framework, allows better response and anticipation of the opportunities and threats.

Learning based organisations grow by retaining and managing knowledge as a key resource. Learning is achieved by individuals becoming empowered to take responsibility for their own learning. The more individuals learn and develop, the greater the prospect of the organisation growing in an appropriate manner. However, the organisations need a framework to retain the individual's learning within the organisation.

One of the primary reasons for the failure of strategies is the management's inability to implement them in an effective and efficient way. A project based approach employing Action Learning Teams ensures that realistic goals are set, with the timing being given due consideration. Completion of actions is closely monitored, with a degree of flexibility being offered to change the plans if required.

Describing an Option

An option should be described as fully as possible with as much specific detail as possible. There is a tendency to keep the definition vague and general, leading to an ineffective evaluation. The core elements of the strategy need to be described as fully as possible.

Considerable emphasis on using storytelling techniques for describing the strategy should be given. This encourages greater detail in the description of an option and a more vivid picture, which can be better communicated to the people involved. One of the reasons for a lack of attachment to chosen strategies is the result of confusion caused by the lack of specificity in the description of the option. Many strategic plans are written as a series of bullet points and quantitative, unexciting figures. This creates little attachment to the strategy, let alone recognition. Storytelling, as part of the communication process, helps in the selling of a strategy.

The key principles of writing a story to assist with the "buy-in" of the strategy are:

- Ensure there is a beginning, a middle and an end
- Introduction – including the background

- Timing – ensure that the reader of the strategy travels at a pace you wish them to
- Scene setting – a timed sequence of the key issues that need to be addressed by the strategy
- Believable – ensure that the description of the strategy is realistic and relevant
- Compelling – understand the emotional elements that the readers can link to, and keep the message simple

Looking for Conflicts in Options

One of the problems discovered in the process of identifying options is that certain options actually have direct conflicts with each other, thus reducing the likelihood of being able to combine options together. Potential sources of conflict that need to be taken into account are:

- Inappropriate staff
- Leadership style
- Expenditure v financial benefit
- Potential clash of cultures
- Inappropriate structure and systems
- Inadequate skills or mismatch of skills

By identifying these conflicts, organisations can harness a variety of options into logical clusters, remembering that you may not implement everything at once, but in steps over a period of time.

Fig. 14.8 and *Fig.14.9* show a format that may be used for clustering the options. The table provides a way of showing the critical levers related to each of the options. The figure shows the permutations of each of the options that are possible.

Clustering Options

Options are not all necessarily mutually exclusive and have a certain degree of fit, which allows different options to be clustered together. However, there may be conflicts in options, which means that two options may not fit together, as stated above.

Option	Critical levers
1	
2	
3	
4	

Fig. 14.8: Critical levers in options

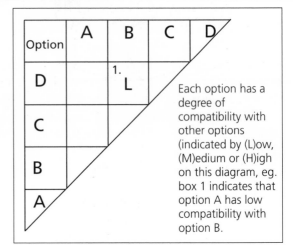

Fig. 14.9: Options mix

Key Steps

1. Summarise the key issues identified in the analysis
2. Create options development team
3. Brainstorm options
4. Identify critical levers of each option
5. Explore different permutations of each option
6. Cluster options into logical groupings
7. Tell the story, describing each of the options

Summary

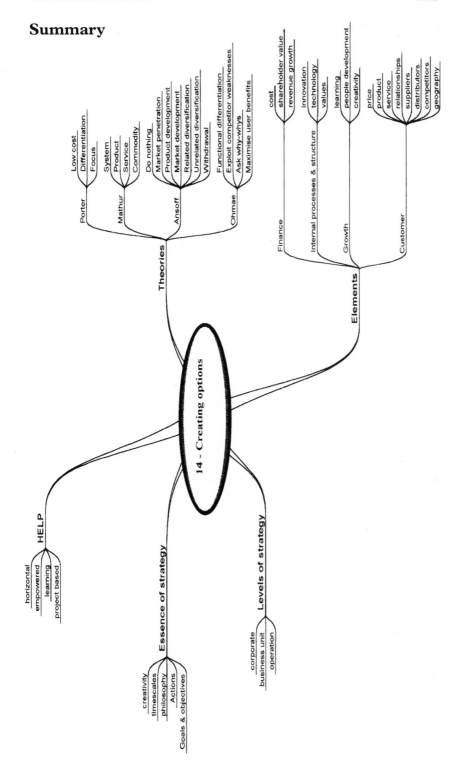

Theories

Porter
Low cost
Differentiation
Focus

Mathur
System
Product
Service
Commodity

Ansoff
Do nothing
Market penetration
Product development
Market development
Related diversification
Unrelated diversification
Withdrawal

Ohmae
Functional differentiation
Exploit competitor weaknesses
Ask why-whys
Maximise user benefits

Elements

Finance
cost
shareholder value
revenue growth

Internal processes & structure
innovation
technology
values

Growth
learning
people development
creativity

Customer
price
product
service
relationships
suppliers
distributors
competitors
geography

14 - Creating options

HELP
horizontal
empowered
learning
project based

Essence of strategy
creativity
timescales
philosophy
Actions
Goals & objectives

Levels of strategy
corporate
business unit
operation

15

CHOOSING OPTIONS

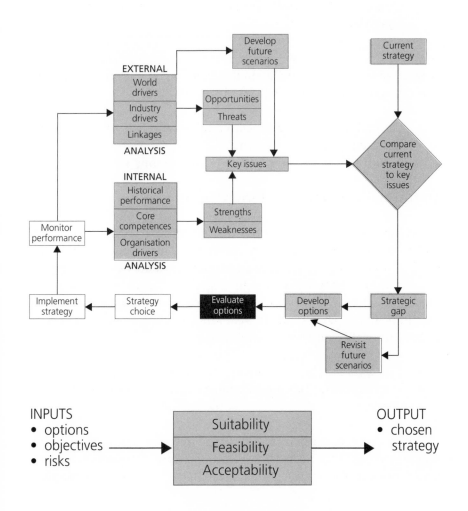

"Attempt nothing beyond your strength. "
Unknown

CONCEPTS

Choosing a Strategy

At its simplest, the process of evaluation should comprise an assessment of the pros and cons of each option in a balanced and non-judgemental way. The process of evaluating the options depends on the:

- Definition of the objectives of the strategy
- Quality of the evaluation method
- Quality of the understanding of the options and their potential outcomes

If we are unclear and have not identified, in a rigorous manner, the issues that need to be satisfied in the analysis, then doing anything is a relevant option. Evaluating options is about:

- Developing the clear objectives of what needs to be achieved
- Identifying relevant options
- Identifying the risks attached to the options

Defining the Purpose of the Option

What purpose is to be served by the option? This is a key question and is sometimes left quite unanswered. This would include the outline objectives of the chosen strategy, which need to be very specific. There may be a certain degree of iteration between the objectives and the ultimate chosen strategy. Nothing needs to be, or should be fixed, particularly in a rapidly changing environment. The statement of the purpose should include:

- The level at which the strategy is aimed
- The limits and boundaries, where relevant, of the chosen strategy

An appropriate method for defining the purpose is to use the earlier mentioned CATOE framework. This will ensure all aspects are clearly stated prior to the options being evaluated. As far as the objectives go, there will be levels of objectives that have to be satisfied, depending on the various stakeholders involved, and need to be represented. These objectives should be prioritised against:

- HIGH – objectives that have to be met by an option
- LOW – objectives that in an ideal world should be met

The list of objectives will also include the issues that have been prioritised and identified as key in the strategic analysis. These should also be prioritised in terms of HIGH and LOW.

Evaluating the Options

Johnson & Scholes in *Exploring Corporate Strategy* suggest using the following framework for evaluating the options – Suitability, Feasibility and Acceptability:

(i) Suitability

To what extent does the option address the issues facing the organisation and address the objectives highlighted earlier in the evaluation process?

Each of the issues and objectives should be listed in order of priority, with the HIGH priorities leading. Each of the options needs to be considered in terms of to what extent they actually address the issues, ranking each of the options in the process.

The key purpose of assessing suitability is to answer the following questions:

- Does the strategy exploit the internal company strengths and external opportunities?
- Does the strategy overcome internal company weaknesses and overcome external threats?
- Does the strategy fit in with the purpose and objectives of the organisation?

(ii) Feasibility

To what extent does the organisation have the financial, physical and human resources to see the strategy through?

The feasibility of a strategy depends on:

- The level of funding required to implement the strategy
- The skills gap that needs to be filled, based on desired versus actual skills requirement
- The technology being available and in place
- Physical resources and facilities, such as buildings, being available.

(iii) Acceptability

To what extent is the strategy acceptable to the key stakeholders?

In addition to determining the acceptability of an option to the stakeholders, consideration needs to be given also to the level of risk attached to each option. Each of the options needs to be further analysed to explore the potential risks attached to them. The consequences of each of the options is a creative exercise requiring a balanced view from all perspectives. Some of the questions that should be asked are:

- Are there any key success criteria that have been missed in the analysis?
- What organisational factors and changes to the current state of the organisation could adversely affect the success of this option?
- What external changes could render this option useless?
- What issues could make implementation of this option extremely difficult?

The types of risk that an organisation is likely to face can be categorised in terms of the reporting criteria within the Balanced Scorecard (see Chapter 17) which are:

- Financial
- Customer
- Internal processes
- Growth and innovation.

This process needs to be applied to the option that at the moment seems to be the most likely to be chosen. Each of the risks can be assessed for see *Fig. 15.1*:

Risks	Probability of occurence (%) (A)	Degree of seriousness (0-10) (B)	(A) x (B)
1. Financial			
2. Customer			
3. Internal Processes			
4. Growth & Innovation			

Fig. 15.1: Risks assessment

- Probability of occurrence – which can be stated as a percentage and asks the question "What is the likelihood of this risk happening?"
- Degree of seriousness – which can be stated on a basis of 1 to 10, and assesses how serious it will be if this risk happens.

The key to this assessment is to be able to identify the high probability, high serious risks during the evaluation process.

Part of the evaluation of the acceptability of a strategic option should investigate the level of financial benefit to be gained from the option. There are many financial methods available, such as Internal Rate of Return, Discounted Cashflow and Net Present Value. However, we shall be making use of a method that has become quite popular in recent times, Strategic Value Analysis (Mills) (ref. 15.1).

Strategic Value Analysis

The core of strategic analysis is the determination of Free cashflow (Fig. 15.2), which is a function of the Cash Inflow and Cash Outflow.

Key drivers are used to express the Strategic Value, as highlighted by Mills. These are:

A. CASH INFLOW

A1. Sales Growth rate
Realistic estimates are made for the likely growth in sales during the life of the strategy. This means converting the strategy into a set of

Ref. 15.1: Mills, R. W. "Strategic Value Analysis", (Mars Business Associates, 1994)

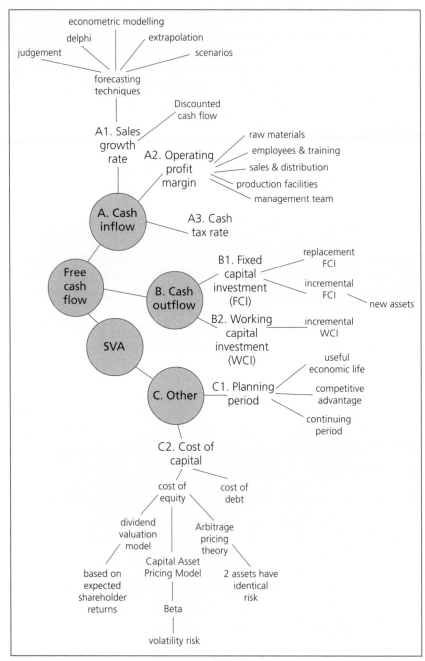

Fig/ 15.2: Strategic value analysis

focused numbers reflecting the likely results of the strategy. Not only are the skills of forecasting paramount, but also an understanding of the likely timing of sales growth. This, once again, demands a good understanding of the dynamics of the business, hence systems thinking. A tendency exists to apply a blanket approach to the growth rates, i.e. a uniform growth rate is applied over the period of the strategy. The strategy should be brought down to individual product and geographical level.

A number of forecasting techniques are available to assist at this stage of the evaluation. Some of these include:

- Causal models – Builds on the notion that organisational performance is linked to activity in the external environment, and in particular the economic factors. By monitoring each of the causal factors, it becomes possible to predict future values for the size of the market. One of the difficulties of this method is the identification of the causal factors, rather than those factors that appear to be the drivers. Examples of techniques used are regression analysis, Monte Carlo Simulation, least squares and correlation.

- Time series analysis – This method incorporates the use of historical data, but has the disadvantage of ignoring signals that may change the future from the past. Typical examples of time series analysis are moving averages and trend analysis.

- Delphi – Experts are consulted for their views about the future. This allows you to take on board a number of views. The advantages of this technique is that it promotes a wide variety of issues to be taken into account, and is an objective view, as the experts are not likely to be influenced by the leaders. The disadvantage of the technique is that the experts are usually quite expensive, and this method is quite time consuming.

In determining the sales growth rate the strategy team has to take into account the fact that there will never be a continuity of growth rates, i.e. a steady growth will not be consistently achieved over the period of the strategy. There will always be discontinuities.

One of the criticisms of planning methods that attempt to ascertain the feasibility and acceptability of a strategy is that they do not take account of likely discontinuities in the environment. Forecasting methods, and in particular, the work on scenarios allow us to consider the uncertainty that is associated with our environment.

Earlier in our analysis we developed possible scenarios with levels of uncertainty associated with possible futures. These scenarios now need to be taken into consideration in our evaluation model, by carrying out a variety of "what if" analyses. These will help us gauge the downside of options if the discontinuities occur in the environment. These occurrences may radically change the outcome of the evaluation. Each of the discontinuities should be listed, and applied to each of the options with a variety of permutations. This allows us to compare the various risks and determine their impact on each of the options. Sensitivity analysis, on this basis, encourages more rigorous decision making.

The use of the Balanced Scorecard to monitor performance allows us to check the key criteria as an early warning system, so that these discontinuities can be picked up early enough. No strategy is likely ever to turn out exactly as it was planned. However, this is not the purpose of strategic planning. Strategic planning allows an organisation to commence taking its first steps, which are appropriate now, towards its thousand mile journey. The system should then be set up to monitor the key variables, as an early warning system, to identify, at an appropriate time, a change in direction. The ultimate aim is to have a strategy of no strategy, where the understanding of the organisation is such that the need for changes are identified early enough and made almost instantly. This can only be achieved if the system is TOTAL.

A2. Operating Profit margin
This is a function of the cost structure of the organisation, which comprises:

- Cost of raw materials
- Employees and training
- Sales and distribution
- Production facilities
- Management team

A3. Cash Tax rate
This allows us to estimate the amount of tax to be paid on our profits, which is why it is shown as a negative cash inflow.

B. CASH OUTFLOW

B1. Fixed capital needs
Comprises two components that need to be quantified when translating a strategy into a set of financial outcomes:

1 Replacement Fixed Capital Investment – the capital requirements to replace existing fixed assets to maintain the current level of activity in the organisation.
2 Incremental Fixed Capital Investment – the capital requirements to grow the fixed assets to reflect the projected growth in the strategy.

B2. Working capital needs
The level of investment required in working capital in items such as stocks, etc.

C. OTHER

C1. Cost of capital
A company has two sources of capital with the associated costs:

1 Cost of Debt – this in essence is the borrowing that takes place from sources such as banks
2 Cost of Equity – this is far more difficult to estimate due to the possible variety in investor needs and expectations. The cost of equity can be determined by a host of complex techniques such as:

• Dividend Valuation Model
• Capital Asset Pricing Model
• Arbitrage Pricing Theory

C2. Planning period
This determines the useful economic life of the strategy, reflecting the scope for achieving the competitive advantage. In addition, the plan and valuation should also reflect that no strategy simply comes to an outright end, unless the organisation dies. There is a period of continuity in the strategy where a certain level of income will continue.

Stakeholder Analysis

Other stakeholders need to be considered in the evaluation process. Stakeholder analysis forces the team to consider the reactions of the people involved in implementing a strategy. Each of the key stakeholders is identified and the forces identified that:

- Support the changes
- Resist the changes

Fig. 15.3 shows a possible format for evaluation of the stakeholder. Fig. 15.4 shows a format for the whole evaluation process.

Option		Stakeholders			
		A	B	C	D
1	For				
	Against				
2	For				
	Against				
3	For				
	Against				

Fig. 15.3: Stakeholder evaluation

Option	Purpose/ priorities	Suitability			Feasibility			Acceptability				
		Issue 1	Issue 2	Issue 3	Financial	Physical	Human	Stakeholders A	B	C	Financial benefits	Risks
1	a.											
	b.											
	c.											
2	a.											
	b.											
	c.											
3	a.											
	b.											
	c.											

Note: Any relevant scoring system may be used to complete the boxes.

Fig. 15.4: Evaluating options

Evaluation

1. List all options
2. List all issues identified in the analysis
3. Compare the options against the issues to determine the level of suitability
4. Identify the resource requirements for each option
5. Identify the level of resources available
6. Determine the level of feasibility of each option
7. Identify the stakeholders and their needs
8. Identify the sources of support and resistance for each of the options
9. Calculate the financial outcomes of each option
10. Build in the discontinuities and carry out "what if" analyses
11. Determine the level of the acceptability of each option
12. Choose an option or range of options (Fig. 15.4)

Summary

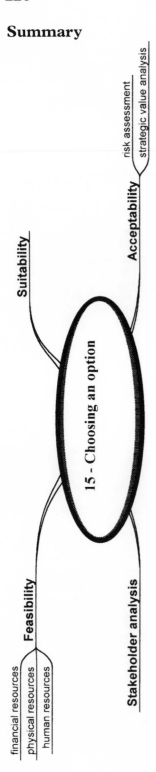

16

MAKING THE STRATEGY WORK

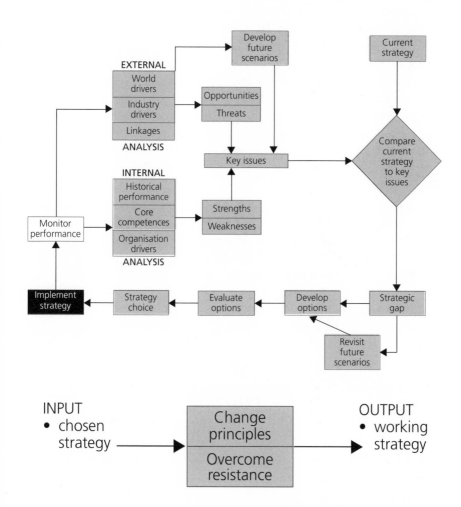

"To the brave and faithful nothing is difficult."
Unknown

CONCEPTS

General

An organisation can be described as the interrelationship of the 7Ss, i.e. strategy, structure, systems, style, shared values, staff and skills. In total these represent a comprehensive representation of the organisation. We looked at each of these elements for the purpose of analysis, to determine the current situation of the organisation (position A in *Fig. 16.1*). The chosen new strategy is represented by position B in *Fig. 16.1*. The purpose of strategy development is to identify the changes in the mix of 7Ss to cope with a changing environment. The basis for McKinsey's 7Ss is that if one of the Ss changes, then, due to the level of interconnectivity, each of the other Ss must also change to some degree. For example, if an organisation changes it organisation structure from a functional to a matrix structure, it also needs to consider the changes to staff, skills, shared values, systems, etc. as these will have been designed for a functional structure. Therefore, any implementation programme needs to take account of the impact of change on each of the 7Ss.

Principles of change

Making the strategy work depends on the process of implementation adopted by the organisation. There are many aspects that need to be addressed, and there are three basic principles to ensure that adequate attention is given to implementation issues:

1. *Fig. 16.1* shows the current situation and the desired situation, i.e. the new strategy. Implementation needs to address the question "how

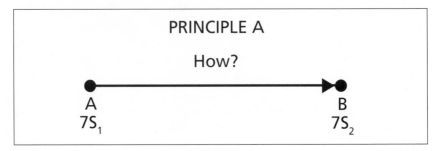

PRINCIPLE A

How?

A
$7S_1$

B
$7S_2$

Fig. 16.1: How to change?

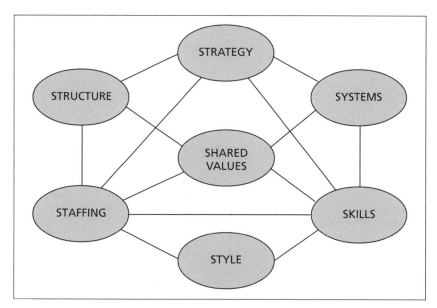

Fig.: 16.2: McKinsey's 7Ss

is the change to be made?" Too often, organisations find themselves restating position B rather than asking themselves, how do we get to B? So principle A of implementation is:

• Focus on how to reach the desired position.

2. Implementation is like Sun Tzu's thousand mile journey, i.e. it starts with the first step! One of the most difficult aspects of implementation is identifying the first step. Many organisations focus on implementing strategy as a series of short term steps *(Fig. 16.3 (i))*. The danger with this approach is that the short term measures take little account of the strategy and are the equivalent of fire fighting measures. These steps tend to be reactions to current problems, rather than addressing the real issues.

Successful implementation demands drive and a passionate belief in the long term. The process of strategy development has to be seen to be fundamental to the success of the organisation and, more important: the strategy needs to drive a change in organisation behaviour. *Fig. 16.3 (ii)* shows that the "first step" needs to be driven backwards from the long term, desired position. Therefore, the establishment of priorities in the short, medium and long term all lead in the same direction, the direction of the selected strategy. Principle B of implementation is:

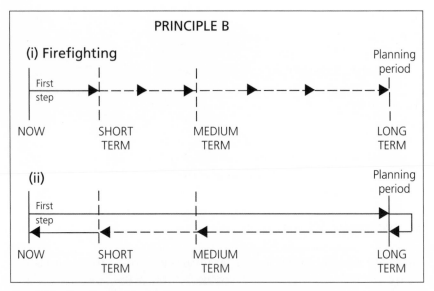

Fig. 16.3: Setting action plans

- Establish the priorities and identify tangible actions in the SHORT, MEDIUM and LONG terms.

3. There tends to be a resistance to change unless desperation sets in. Unfortunately, "comfortable" organisations sometimes fail to see the need to change when things are going well. To start the change process, organisations need to find a way of creating some form of chaos, or movement, in the organisation which will then make the process of change more fluid.

The initial step in the process of change is the creation of instability in the organisation, thus generating a greater desire to make the implementation process work. In 1998, BA announced huge profits and at the same time announced 5,000 job cuts! This instability creates a more fluid organisation, and when the staff become comfortable with this type of culture there tends to be an increased awareness and sense of purpose within the organisation.

One of the dangers in a dynamic and complex environment is that the organisation becomes too comfortable and arrogant, and creates an air of stability or, to a large extent, a state of ignorance. Therefore, it is recommended that the aim should be to create a flexible organisation that is constantly in a state of "controlled chaos", which perhaps should become a key part of the corporate culture. This state of controlled chaos acts as a stimulus for creativity, as it is a form of positive tension, which ultimately ensures peak performance. Principle C of implementation is:

- Create a state of "controlled chaos".

To summarise, the three key principles of implementation are:

1 Focus on how to reach the desired position.
2 Establish the priorities and identify the tangible actions in the short, medium and long terms.
3 Create a state of "controlled chaos".

Overcoming Resistance

All major and minor change programmes face resistance from some quarters. Management needs to understand the reasons for the resistance and identify appropriate ways of handling these problems. There is a tendency for a small number, maybe around 10%, of people who support the change programme in a fervent and enthusiastic manner. These people tend to be involved in the strategy building process. On the other hand, there is a similar number of people who are fully against the change programme. The remainder, around 80%, usually "sit on the fence" waiting for the most vocal to make its views known. In such circumstances there is a tendency for management to "fight" the people who are against the changes, thus fuelling the antagonism and "forcing" the majority to tip over to the side of the forces against change. However, if management attempted to support the people resisting change through greater communication and "friendly" open discussion, there is a greater likelihood of the majority becoming more accepting of the change programme, over a period of time. Certain people will have personal motives – these need to be discovered and dealt with in a positive manner.

Fig. 16.4 discusses some of the more typical problems causing resistance and how these may be overcome.

Emotional Gateways of Change

One of the keys to overcoming resistance to change, in strategy implementation, is to have an understanding of the changing emotions individuals go through in any change situation. The

Factor	Overcoming the factor
1. Unclear aims	Set realistic aims that inspire people
2. Unclear values	Create a matching of personal and corporate values
3. Inappropriate management style	Leadership and style is appropriate for the situation
4. Poor management development and training	Managers possess relevant competencies
5. Unsuitable organisation structure	Structure is tied into strategy
6. Poor control	Correct measures are monitored and rewards reflect performance
7. Unfair rewards	Reward system encourages high performance
8. Poor communication	Communication is consistent and effective in all directions
9. Low motivation	Employees are committed to the organisation
10. Poor teamwork	People enjoy working together in teams

Fig. 16.4: Factors causing resistance to change

Emotional Gateways of Change are shown in *Fig. 16.5*. The first stage people go through, on instigation of a major change, is shock. People speak of being speechless, unable to think straight and acting in a state of numbness. This state can manifest itself in many different ways. Some individuals go into a state of total silence, while others act in fits of rage, becoming very violent.

The second stage is a state of denial. Individuals cannot believe this is happening to them and think it is all a bad dream, that the situation will revert to "normal" once they awaken. Obviously, things never do go back to the way they were.

The third stage of the cycle is acceptance and acknowledgement that the change is happening and that this now needs to be taken into account when thinking of the future. At this stage the implementation programme needs to begin to take advantage of changing attitudes to speed up the process of change.

Finally, the fourth stage reflects the individual adapting to the "new world" and trying to fit in with the changing environment.

Clearly, it is essential that due consideration is given to these stages of the emotional cycle in any strategy plan that is developed. Strategists need to accept that people cannot be rushed through each stage, and ensure that there is a deep enough understanding of the people, in an organisation for account to be taken of different

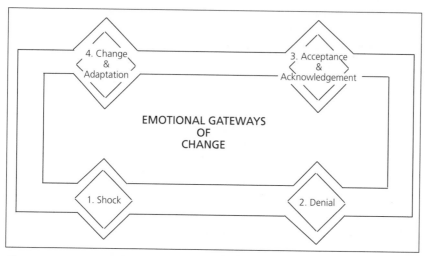

Fig. 16.5: The emotional gateways of change

individuals. Many organisations that do not give ample consideration to this issue find that in the process of rushing the change programme, they actually build an increased resistance that ultimately stops the change from happening. The aim being to get all staff through all four gates as quickly and safely as possible.

The skills of the leader need to include empathy building, which allows the leader to take account of the varying needs of individuals.

Forcefield Analysis

Forcefield analysis explores the deeper motivations for change. Its real value is in helping to prevent or minimise conflict. Forcefield analysis is applied in situations presenting pressure to change. The forces driving change are identified as well as the forces restraining change.

There is always considerable resistance to change. Understanding the drivers and restraining forces helps facilitate change. Practice has shown that there is a pareto effect in that 80% of the restraining is done by 20% of the restraining forces, and 80% of the driving is done by 20% of the driving forces. Therefore, it is essential that the forces are prioritised so that the key forces are addressed.

The key steps in carrying out a forcefield analysis are as follows:

1 Identify the stakeholders who will be influenced by the change process
2 Brainstorm forces driving the change
3 Brainstorm forces restraining the change
4 Plot and review forces on the diagram below.

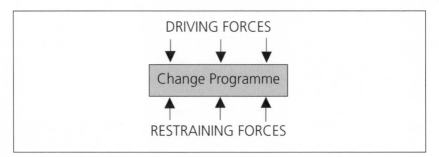

Fig. 16.6: Forcefield analysis

The process to determine the current state would be as follows:

1 Prepare a statement of the desired state in terms of behaviour of the different stakeholders.
2 Identify the role of different stakeholder groups and their motivating interests.
3 Allocate scores for the importance of having the support of each stakeholder, e.g. a score of 10 suggests that it is vital you have the complete support of the stakeholder, a score of 0 suggests that the change can be implemented without this stakeholder's support.
4 Determine the attitude of each stakeholder towards the change programme. *Fig. 16.7* shows a possible scoring mechanism.
5 Multiply the scores for importance and attitude to determine the significance of the stakeholder *(Fig. 16.8)*.
6 Investigate and identify the cross-relationships between each pair of roles.

Behaviour	Score
Active resistance	-2
Passive resistance	-1
Indifferent	0
Co-operation	1
Enthusiastic support	2

Fig. 16.7: Attitude scoring system

Stakeholder	Importance of stakeholder	Attitude of stakeholder	Significance of stakeholder
	(0 to 10)	(-2 to +2)	
(A)	(B)	(C)	(B) * (C)

Fig. 16.8: Stakeholder significance

Project Management

Project Management techniques are relevant for all major change projects. They ensure that the implementation of change is successful in terms of on-time performance and in terms of financial criteria. It also ensures that all members of the team are geared towards achieving common goals and objectives as highlighted in the new strategy.

A project management culture encourages flexibility in the implementation, while focusing on delivering the desired outputs. The five objectives of utilising a project approach are accurately to determine the:

- Scope
- Time
- Cost
- Quality
- Organisation

needed to implement a strategy successfully.

At the strategic level, the project should clearly define goals and milestones, and the allocation of responsibility for the key stages of the implementation programme. This helps considerably in the prioritisation of activities.

At the tactical level, activities required to achieve the milestones and allocating the tasks to individual team members are essential. There are many good texts on project management that should be explored.

The creation of a project-based organisation for the successful implementation of strategic change programmes is achieved by:

1　Assign priority to development work
2　Make a contract between operations and project managers
3　Formalise resource requirements
4　Give visibility to plans
5　Adopt a company wide approach to project management
6　Educate all personnel in its use.

Certain pitfalls exist in the implementation of projects:

1. Projects

Some of the common pitfalls in the project itself focus on misalignment of the project plans with the business plans. This may be due to the lack of involvement and communication of project managers with the strategic planning process. Consequently there is no shared vision and significant internal conflict.

2. Planning

Project planning is always in danger of adopting unfriendly tools that fail to communicate the objectives effectively. Too much focus on technicalities discourages creativity, which makes implementation very difficult.

3. Organising and Implementing

Poor communication leads to a lack of co-operation, and also unclear management responsibility.

4. Control

A common cause of failure in implementation occurs when plans and progress reports are not fully integrated and the review process is not fully formalised. Without control and monitoring, team members tend to lose direction.

Good project management entails attention to:

- Organisation
- People issues
- Planning and control systems
- External influences
- Financing the project
- Scheduling the project.

Summary

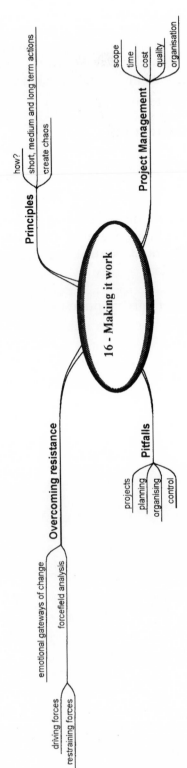

Principles
  how?
  short, medium and long term actions
  create chaos

Project Management
  scope
  time
  cost
  quality
  organisation

16 - Making it work

Pitfalls
  projects
  planning
  organising
  control

Overcoming resistance
  emotional gateways of change
  forcefield analysis
    driving forces
    restraining forces

17

LIVING TOTAL STRATEGY

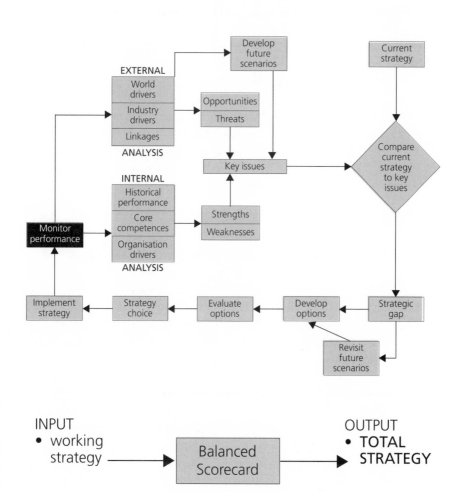

"If you cannot measure it, you cannot control it."
Unknown

CONCEPTS

The old adage that if you cannot measure it, you cannot control it is fundamental to ensuring the strategy is implemented successfully. Measurement of performance ensures that strategy lives in the organisation and that everyone is working towards the common goals of the organisation. Measuring valid factors also convinces team members of the need for change. As progress is monitored and communicated, the desire for seeing further improvements increases. However, certain rules have to be observed:

1. Measures are consistent with strategic aims.

2. All members have measurable aims that contribute to the corporate whole.

If these are not possible for any individual, questions need to be asked as to whether that position contributes anything worthwhile to the corporate whole. Note it may be that management is not fully seeing the potential of the position and position holder.

3. Measures should be monitored consistently and regularly.

4. Results should be open and well communicated.

5. Reward systems should be designed around the measures.

The establishment of performance criteria translates directly into personal priorities, which in turn are converted into corporate values and culture. In this dynamic environment it is not enough just to focus on the financial parameters. Though the financial measures are vital, they sometimes can be achieved at the expense of factors that are more likely to contribute to long term sustainable growth, such as factors affecting employees. Some organisations do very well at measuring financial measures, but can this level of performance be sustained, and can the organisation say it is maximising its potential?

Other factors that should be taken into account are:

- Meeting customer expectations
- Improving the way things are done
- Helping staff to grow through learning

Each of these factors impacts on the organisation's potential to grow in the future. These parameters also represent the core elements of the strategy of the organisation. In essence, four parameters form the system of the strategy of the organisation, and as such are all likely to affect each other. The more you try to meet the increasing expectations of the customer in an effective and efficient manner, by keeping the staff motivated, the greater the impact on the financial results of the organisation *(Fig. 17.1)*.

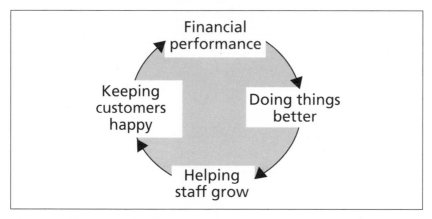

Fig. 17.1: The snowball of performance

Kaplan and Norton (ref. 17.1) devised the Balanced Scorecard as a means of ensuring organisations monitored parameters other than just the financial *(Fig. 17.2)*. They called the different parameters "perspectives". The four perspectives are:

1. The Financial Perspective

One of the major pressures on business managers is the delivery of financial expectations, consistently, to aid growth in the business. These measures summarise the economic consequences of the operational actions that have been taken. Examples of measures covered under the financial perspective are: ROCE, cashflow, profitability, reliability of performance, shareholder value.

Ref. 17.1: Kaplan, R. S. and Norton, D. P., "The Balanced Scorecard", (Harvard Business School Press, 1996)

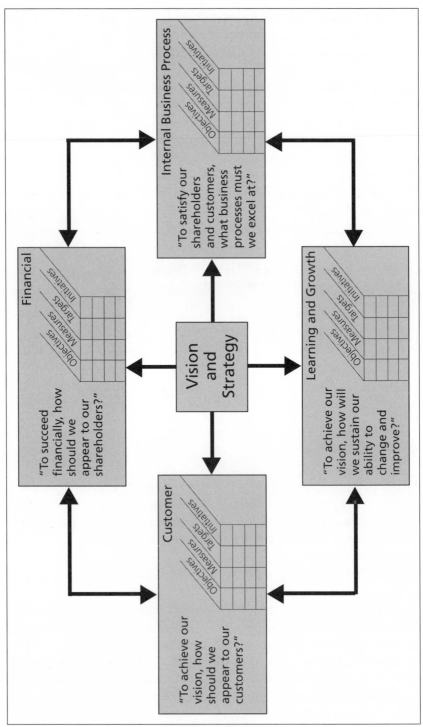

Fig. 17.2: The balanced scorecard provides a framework to translate strategy into operational terms (ref. 17.1)

2. The Customer Perspective

The customer perspective relates to the degree of satisfaction of the specific customer needs of the business and market segments in which the organisation decides to compete. Examples are: value for money, satisfaction, price.

3. The Internal Perspective

These are the processes that the organisation must excel in to be successful in delivering the financial results by satisfying customer needs in the most effective way. These processes will mirror the value chain activities identified in the analysis. Examples are: tender effectiveness, quality, process improvement.

4. The Growth Perspective

Growth occurs through the setup that needs to be built to create long term, sustainable growth. This perspective is often neglected due to the emphasis on short term goals. After all, these can be achieved by discarding the longer term issues. This also explains the lack of focus and cynicism towards longer term strategies being employed. Examples are: empowered workforce, learning, innovation.

The balanced scorecard is a mechanism for translating a company's strategic objectives into a relevant set of performance measures. It does not prescribe a list of factors or measures, but it does provide a focus. The actual measures are dependent on each organisation.

Customised scorecards fit the
- Mission
- Strategy
- Technology
- Culture

of the organisation. *Fig. 17.3* shows the various stages of creating the balanced scorecard. Depending on the nature of the business, there may be other perspectives that need to be taken into account. For example, an airline's balanced scorecard might look like *Fig. 17.4*, where it needs to take into account the safety and security perspective, and the environment and the community. These are key measures that can affect the success of an airline.

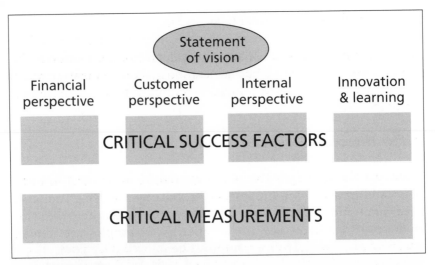

Fig. 17.3: The balanced scorecard

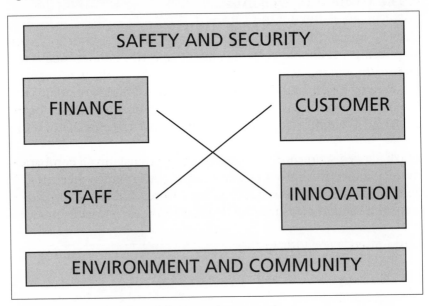

Fig. 17.4: Example of an airline's goal scorecard

The balanced scorecard is set up to influence learning as opposed to being a vehicle to impose control. The focus is on highlighting the areas that an organisation should develop and not to inform management of non-achievement. Its intention is to provide strategic feedback, enhancing the shared vision of the team. Any monitoring system should encourage an openness and discourage fear, as a major input to gaining commitment from the team members to the selected strategy.

One of the major errors of control and monitoring systems is that the measures lack any concept of time. One of the advantages of the balanced scorecard is that the measures contain perspectives that cater for the current term and the short, medium and long terms.

A number of organisations have adopted a balanced scorecard, but there are also a number that have adopted the scorecard but not embraced its philosophy, i.e. they still give precedence to the financial measures. There is little point in an organisation using the balanced scorecard if it is not used fully. It creates additional work and can take an organisation away from the focus it truly desires.

In embracing the method, presentation of data is very important. *Fig. 17.5* shows a method of displaying the results. Each of the perspectives will achieve a proportion of the goal set in a specific period of time. For example, if an organisation achieves all of its financial targets then it has achieved 100%, i.e. 5 out of 5. If it has

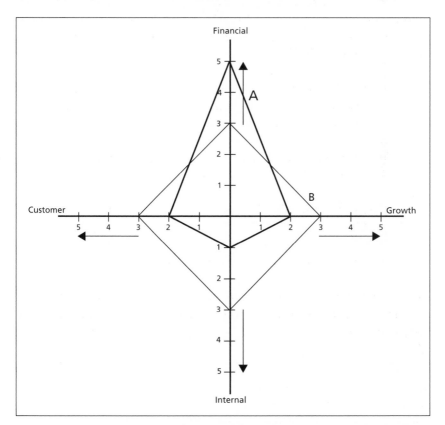

Fig. 17.5: Balanced scorecard reporting

achieved only 60% of target then it will have scored 3 out of 5. These ratios can be plotted on *Fig. 17.5*. Quadrant A demonstrates that the organisation has achieved its financial targets, but at the expense of the other, non-financial targets. This should highlight to the company that balanced performance is not being achieved. Perhaps the target of the organisation in this instance should be to achieve quadrant B. Once B is achieved, then perhaps it should aim to pull all parameters towards their targets together.

Activity 10

List possible measures that might be included in a balanced scorecard for an insurance company.

Reports

A brief word on reporting performance. The format adopted will show whether the issues addressed are understood by everyone in the organisation. *Fig. 17.6* shows a four-part report which can be shown on one page.

- Part A shows the overall level of performance being achieved against whatever format is desired. This could be the balanced scorecard summary.

- Part B identifies the key problem areas that are responsible for the overall corporate performance.

- Part C analyses the drivers that are causing the key problems.

- Part D identifies the key actions needed to rectify the issues.

This format is comprehensive and ensures that key issues are recognised early and acted upon effectively by everyone in the organisation.

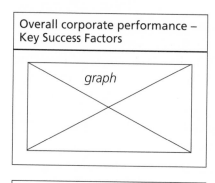

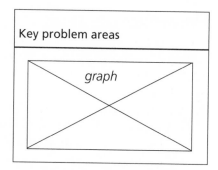

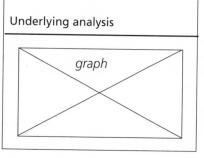

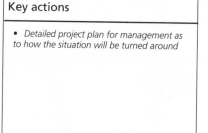

Figure 17.6: Business report format

Solution to Activity 10

Financial
- Return on equity
- Catastrophic losses
- Premium growth

Customer
- Acquisition/retention
- Customer satisfaction

Internal
- Staff turnover
- Loss ratio
- Claims frequency
- Expense ratio
- Develop target markets

Learning
- Staff development
- Training programmes

Summary

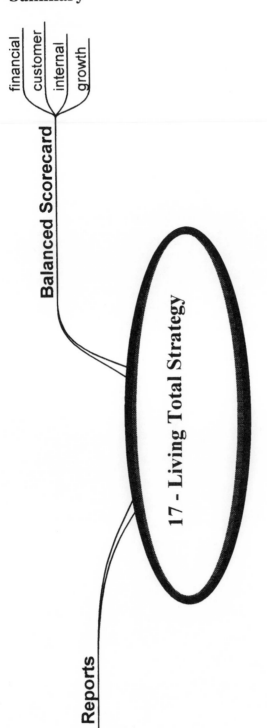

financial
customer
internal
growth

Balanced Scorecard

17 - Living Total Strategy

Reports